Christine Corday

# RELATIVE POINTS

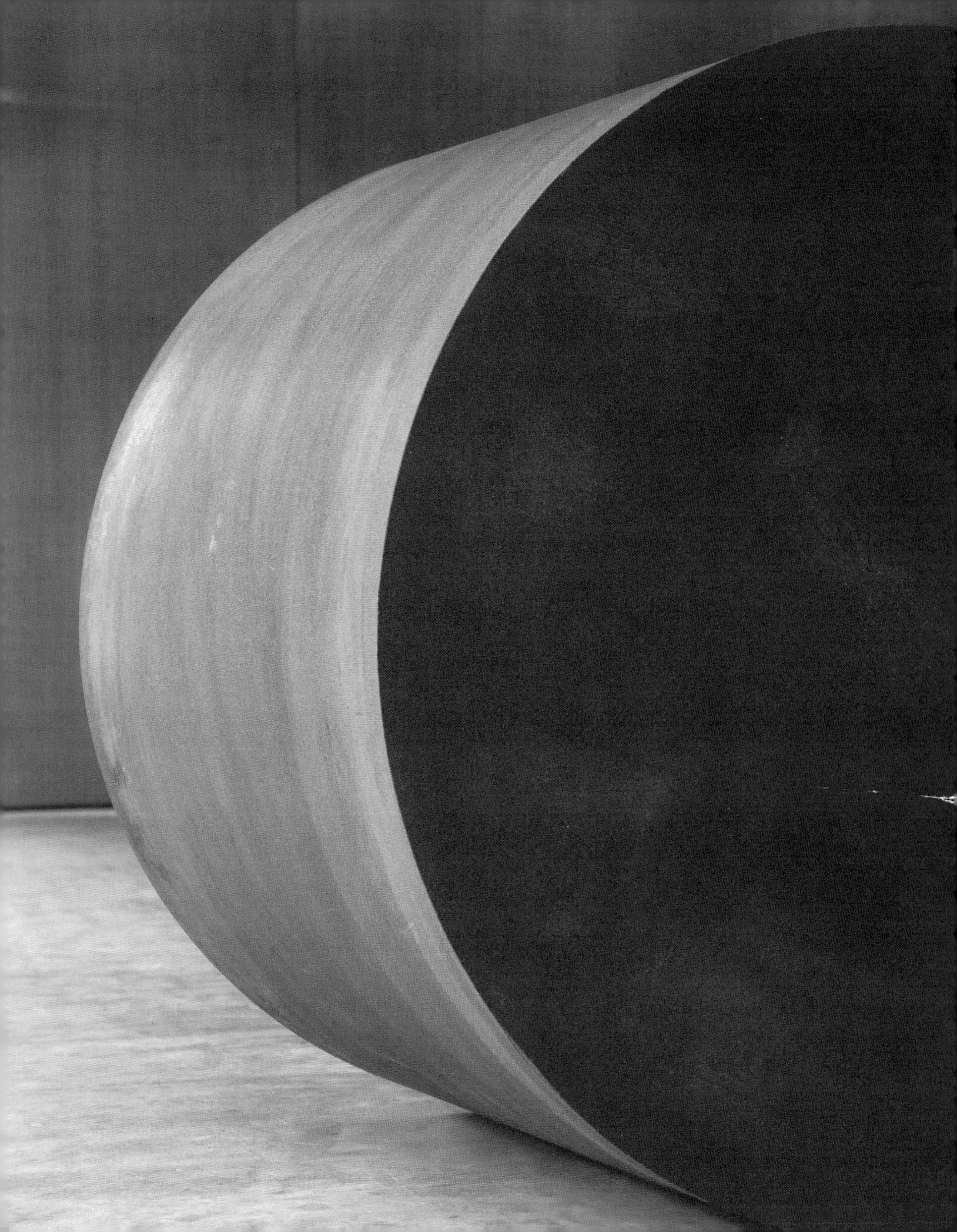

# Christine Corday
# RELATIVE POINTS

Lisa Melandri
Contemporary Art Museum St. Louis

This publication is made possible by the generosity of Barrett Barrera Projects. Our deepest gratitude for your unwavering support.

# Contents

# Foreword and Acknowledgments

Christine Corday combines the sciences with the fine arts to create a unique body of work that investigates space and the universe materially and conceptually. Her site-specific installation at Contemporary Art Museum St. Louis (CAM) is anchored by *RELATIVE POINTS*, a twelve-piece installation of monumental works, and the painting series *Primer Grey, Centers for Gravity*. Each of the *RELATIVE POINTS* is fashioned through a cold-cast process compressing 10,000 pounds of elemental iron metal and metalloid grit into pointed cylindrical forms. These sculptures inhabited CAM's galleries in a non-random constellation where each point was directed toward the center of a centerless—or infinite—cosmos. *RELATIVE POINTS* were made explicitly to be touched. The subtle friction of a visitor's hand ever so slightly changes the surface of these massive works, revealing the power of human interaction. The *Primer Grey* paintings are conceived to complement the dense black forms. The smooth, grey, rectangular planes appear to float weightless on the wall, but each demonstrates a paint buildup on the bottom right pointing out the gravitational pull toward the core of the Earth.

The installation transformed the galleries in ways both minimal and expansive. *RELATIVE POINTS* appear simple in form, belying the complexity of construction and conception. Upon first glance, they seem uniformly black, but subtle variations of warmer tones and values are revealed in the shifting natural light of the museum. Their surfaces are unique and highly differentiated. Some display the marks of their compression, looking like rings on a tree trunk or a galaxy or a mountain range. Visitors described them as both otherworldly—as though deposited in the museum from outer space—and decidedly earthbound—reminding them of hay bales dotting a harvested field. But perhaps most striking was the draw to touch them. The work's monumental scale calls for the presence of the body. Interaction completes Corday's work and viewers became active participants. From light touch to insistent caress to leaning and draping their bodies on the works, visitors to the exhibition realized a tactile relationship with *RELATIVE POINTS*.

For an exhibition such as this, details regarding fabrication and installation are as important as the final display in the museum. Corday experimented with the "recipe" for *RELATIVE POINTS* tirelessly over a two-year period. It was conceptually essential that the works be made with the highest possible percentage of pure iron, but shape, weight, cost, method, and technique had to be carefully considered in order to achieve the goal. As her first show inside a museum, Corday's vision had to be calibrated and tempered to the limits of the doors, lifts, and loads at CAM. I am awestruck by her dogged curiosity and spirit of inquiry. It was a privilege to work with an artist for whom artistic process and production are akin to scientific investigation.

From construction to installation, Corday worked closely with her partner in art and in life, Christopher Powers. His knowledge and understanding of art and architecture fabrication is unparalleled. Although the majority of Corday's works are created in the studio, *RELATIVE POINTS* were cold-compressed in the foundry of Jack Palmer, whose sensitive responsiveness to the artist's instructions in the making of these works is deeply appreciated.

Placing twelve 10,000-pound objects in the museum took a skilled team of thinkers and doers. I am thankful to our excellent and intrepid staff at CAM and particularly indebted to registrars Jessi Cerutti and Jen Nugent, chief curator Wassan Al-Khudhairi, and assistant curator Misa Jeffereis for their extraordinary thoughtfulness, thoroughness, and inventiveness. I would also like to thank John Colurciello, Chris Lucas, Caleb Hauck, and Jamie Wiechens for their deft installation.

We are delighted to publish the accompanying catalog, the first monograph on Corday's work. Michael Govan, CEO and Wallis Annenberg Director, Los Angeles County Museum of Art, worked with Corday to realize an installation of two major sculptures on the LACMA campus in 2014. He understands the power of the work and its context within an art historical trajectory. We are grateful for his astute contribution to this volume. Lisa Le Feuvre, Executive Director, Holt/Smithson Foundation, conducted an interview with the artist that allows us extraordinary insight into Corday's practice in form and materiality, and into her underlying conceptual framework. My great thanks go to Lucia | Marquand for their editorial insight and production, and to Meghann Ney for her handsome design. My appreciation to Jordan Gaunce for his precise post-production work.

This exhibition and catalog could not have been realized without the support of Susan Barrett, Barrett Barrera Projects, and projects+gallery. Barrett has been a champion of Corday's art and was instrumental in allowing her to undertake this body of work, which marks a new direction in Corday's oeuvre. We are exceedingly thankful for her vision and her generosity.

I wish to extend my gratitude to the National Endowment for the Arts for their support. My thanks as well to Penny Pennington and Michael Fidler, and Alexandria and Peter Strelow. Additional support was provided by Ann Ruwitch and John Fox Arnold, and the Robert Lehman Foundation, who underwrote my conversation with Corday at CAM.

There are a host of others whose time, attention, and expertise were essential in bringing the show to fruition, among them Terry Hoffmann, Maryanne Ellison Simmons and Wildwood Press, Paul Henry McMahill, and George Murello. Special thanks to Jeff Hartz for bringing Corday's phenomenal artwork to my attention several years ago.

I have already mentioned the privilege of working with Corday. To that I add heartfelt gratitude for her generosity of spirit, for her breadth of knowledge, and for keeping her eyes toward the stars. It has been an honor to organize this exhibition and to share her brilliant work through this publication.

Lisa Melandri
Executive Director

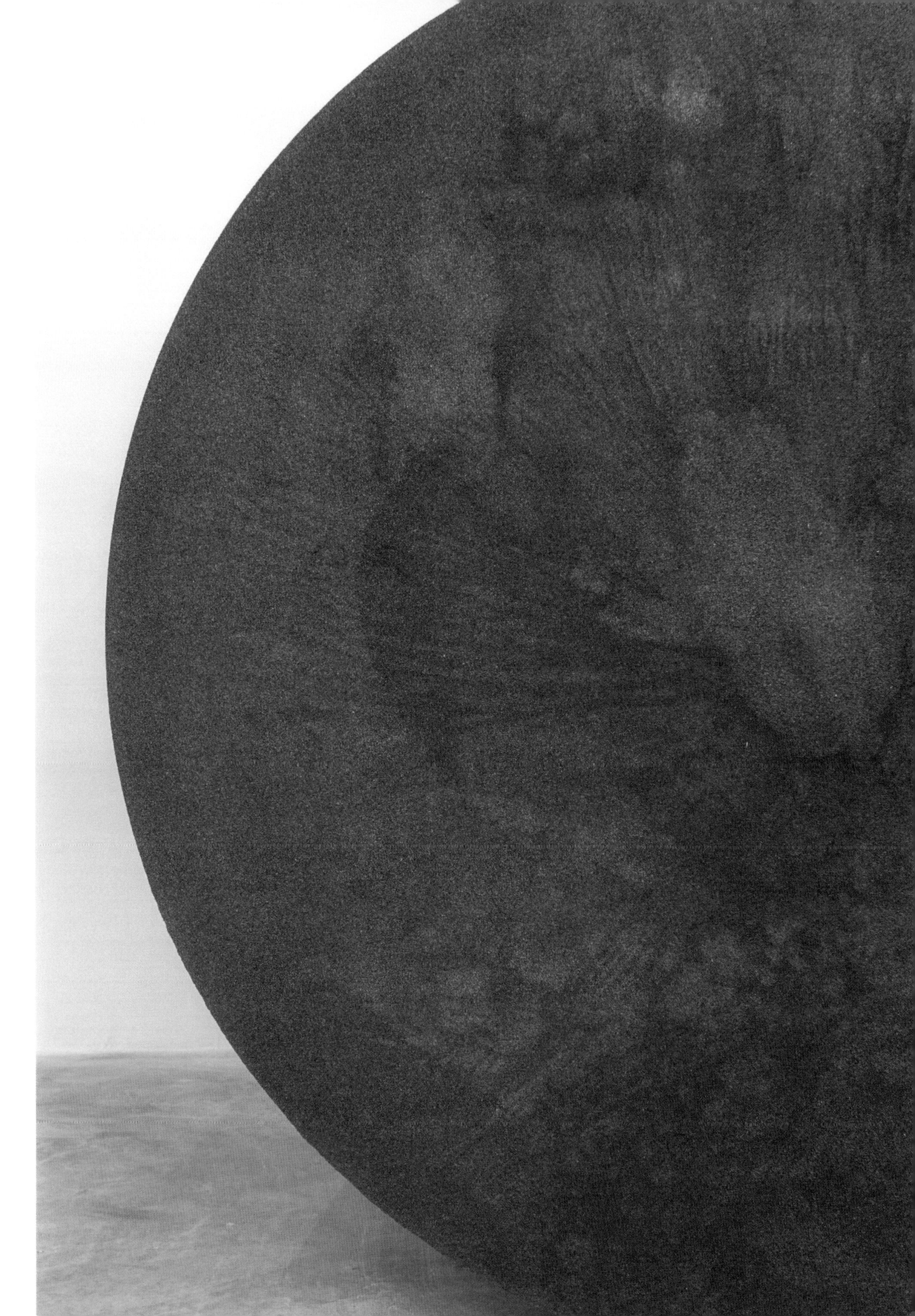

# Material Points

Lisa Melandri

A 21st-century alchemist, Christine Corday plays with materiality and engages with the transformation of matter. She is best known for her large-scale sculptures commissioned for public spaces. For her exhibition at Contemporary Art Museum St. Louis (CAM), Corday presents two new bodies of work that combine art and astrophysics to explore matter and the universe. *RELATIVE POINTS* is an installation of twelve monumental, cold-cast sculptures, created by compressing 10,000 pounds of elemental metal and metalloid grit into a pointed cylindrical form. *Primer Grey, Centers for Gravity* is a painting series in which the artist primes a metal surface and collects the grey primer in the lower corner of the rectangle, indicating the gravitational pull toward the Earth's core.

*RELATIVE POINTS* evidences a significant evolution of Corday's work. As her first exhibition inside a museum, Corday has adapted her formal language and shifted her conceptual framework in order to fit—physically and metaphorically—into the space of the galleries.

*RELATIVE POINTS* are solid, closed forms. Most of Corday's past works are open forms that curve or jut into space. In some sculptures, the planes have been folded, bowed, or bent. But these works are simultaneously cylinders and cubes, dense black masses. When describing the forms, Corday has discussed how they can be seen not only through a number of geometries but also in several dimensions. One end of each *RELATIVE POINT* exhibits a two-dimensional flat circle. The dimensions of each, 53 inches by 53 inches, represent a square, but as each is a sculptural form, also a three-dimensional cube. She describes the barrel-like, cylindrical form of each as a representation of a flat surface that is curved and folded around the circle, implying movement through space—a rolling plane. And Corday takes us even further—one end of each sculpture is a shallow point, a directional signal through time and space. These heavy, dense, inert objects surprisingly point us toward movement into a fourth dimension.

In addition, they are serial—twelve of them grace CAM's galleries, whereas her past monumental sculpture has been decidedly singular. Their seriality is essential to their conceptual framework. The points proliferate to better call out multiple trajectories. Corday has angled each point toward the center of the universe, in what appears to be an arbitrary orientation. In designing this non-random constellation of sculptures, Corday underscores the fundamental idea that the center of the universe is everywhere and nowhere—that "center" is a relative notion. She offers a Zen koan, "If we find comfort with the notion of center, then we must find comfort in a center found in every direction." She asks us to consider ourselves as part of the fabric of the universe right alongside these dense beings. By encouraging us to consider the relationship of our bodies

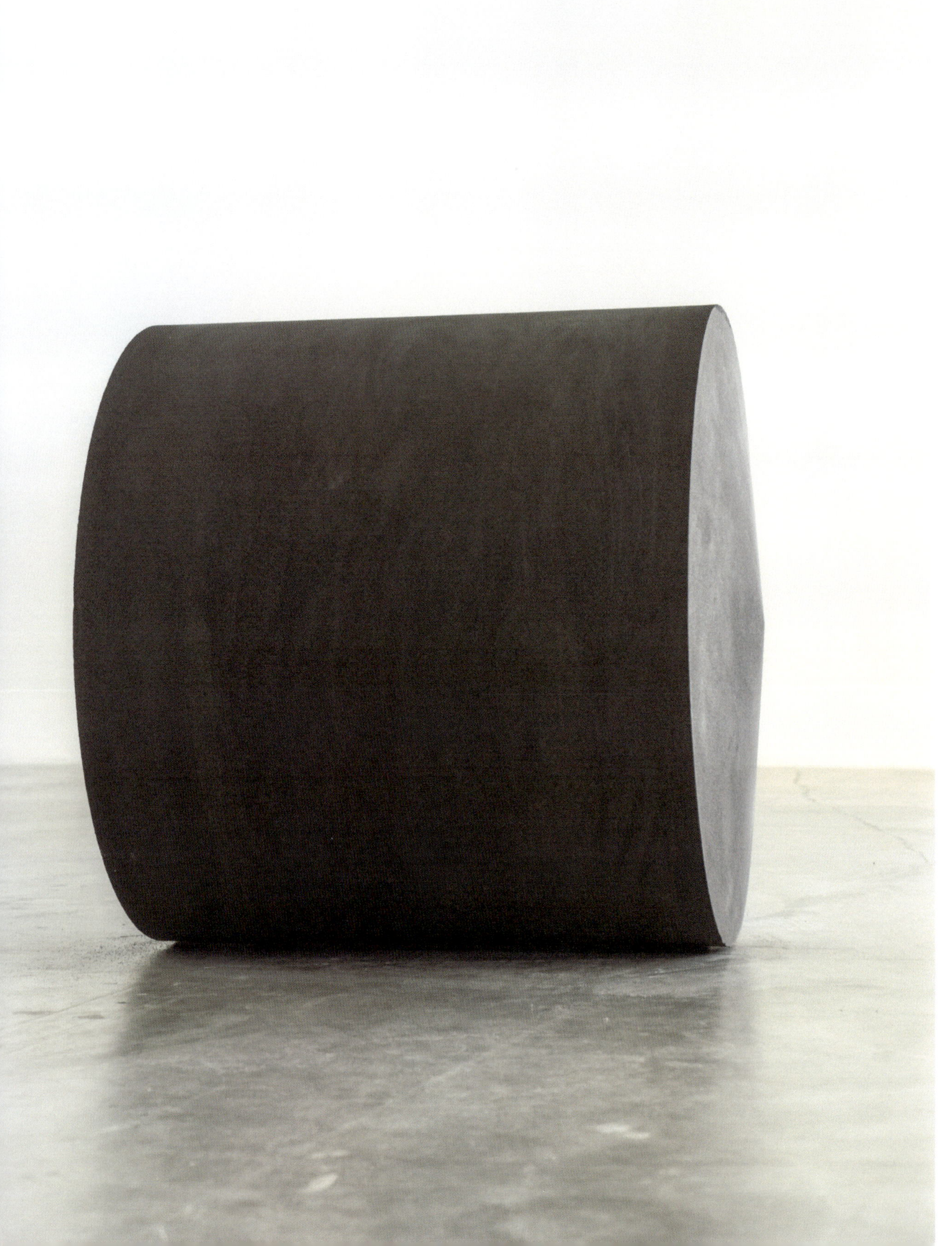

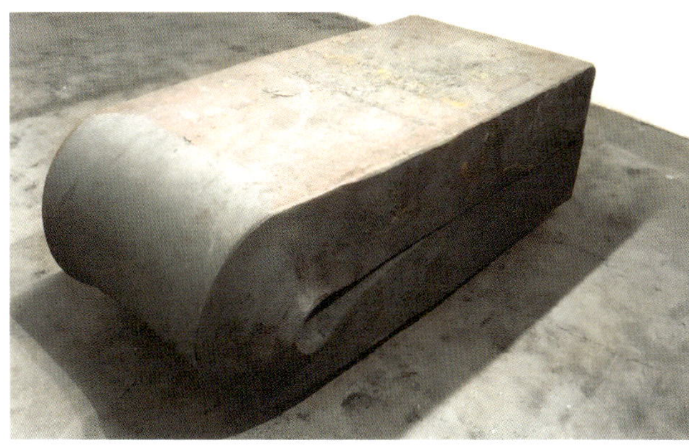

Christine Corday
*+2150F 6500000p*
2017
Elemental metal
20 × 63 × 30 in.
Photo: Jessica Baran

to the sculpture, she encourages us to situate our bodies in the cosmos. Central to Corday's practice is the notion that we are not separate from outer space, but rather we are "absolutely positively in outer space."

*RELATIVE POINTS* are fabricated differently from Corday's previous works. She has long described herself as a heat seeker. Her investigations into creating metal forms have allowed her to brandish tools that function at the temperature of the surface of the sun. When she uses molds, she works with liquefied metal at similar temperatures. The *RELATIVE POINTS*, however, are formed with cold compression. No heat of any kind is applied to the material. Instead, pure force is used to meld the millions of metal grains and metalloid shards into the compact final form. But heat is still present, supplied here by visitors to the exhibition. We transfer the heat of our hands and our bodies to the surface of each *RELATIVE POINT*. Touching the sculpture is required to complete the work and bring a relatively modest 98.5 degrees to the surface. Even though this may seem insignificant, our body temperature exerts power: each touch loosens the very outer layer of grit, sloughing off a bit of the surface as a consequence of subtle friction produced by human contact.

The idea of the viewer as necessary to complete an artwork is certainly not unfamiliar, but it does differentiate Corday's oeuvre from many of its minimalist predecessors working at a monumental scale. Her lexicon of form especially calls to mind Richard Serra, Donald Judd, and Mark di Suvero. But whether in public or private spaces, Corday's objects are created explicitly for interaction. From *RELATIVE POINTS* to the 30-foot-tall *GENESES*, all are made to be touched, handled, and laid and walked upon. CAM offers a particularly advantageous site for Corday's first museum exhibition. Adjacent to CAM's galleries sits Serra's *Joe*, a massive torqued ellipse that is part of the permanent collection of

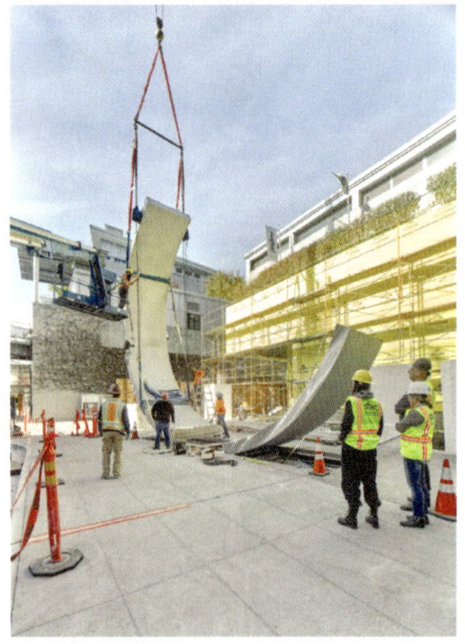

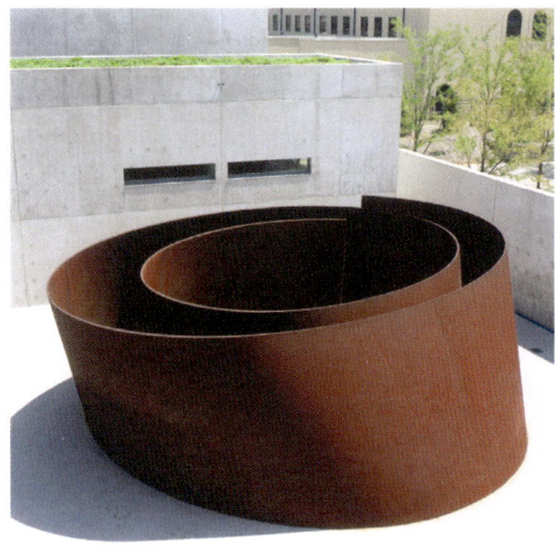

Christine Corday
*GENESES*, installation view, Civic Collection at Howard/4th Moscone Center North Plaza, San Francisco
2019
Stainless steel
360 × 384 × 79 in.
Photo: César Rubio Photography

Richard Serra
*Joe*
1999
Weathering steel
Outer spiral approximately 163 × 576 × 480 in.
Pulitzer Arts Foundation
Photo: Robert Pettus


the neighboring Pulitzer Arts Foundation. *Joe* is visible from numerous vantage points within CAM, and serves as both complement and foil.

A desire for interactivity is not the only link to the human body in Corday's work. There is a long history of large-scale metal sculpture, mostly steel, in art history. While steel contains mostly iron in its make-up, *RELATIVE POINTS* are made specifically and explicitly from the highest possible percentage of pure iron. This choice of material links the cosmos to the Earth to our anatomy. Iron is in the core of stars, in the mantle of the Earth, and in ourselves—each of us contains approximately four grams of iron in our bodies. This work manifests a literal connection between the macro and the micro, between the solar system and the circulatory system. Iron is powerful—it is the element that can cause the explosion of a star, even as it courses peacefully through our bodies. Corday's work is deeply concerned with the human and humanistic, a point often belied by its seemingly inorganic makeup.

In this volume, Michael Govan rightly suggests that Corday's work is not scaled for the collector's living room. Although this is practically true, Corday would in fact love to see a *RELATIVE POINT* or a sculpture from her *Protoist* series inhabit domestic space alongside us in lieu of the couch, table, or armchair. She would want these objects to be at home with us, living with us despite their magnificent size and weight.

*Primer Grey*, *Centers for Gravity* appear to float on the walls of the gallery and offer a light, flat, complement to *RELATIVE POINTS*. These paintings on aluminum supports recast and redefine the monochrome. Corday's minimalism is

Christine Corday
*Primer Grey, Centers for Gravity 5-1*
2018
Primer paint on aluminum
10 × 8 in.
Photo: Dusty Kessler

equally tied to material as to form. Primer is both a color and a material—a kind of conceptual play in which Corday takes delight. She purposefully combines a pristine, seemingly machine-made surface with a mark of the artist's hand. The accretion at the bottom right edge of each work is unique. Sometimes it appears as though the paint has been dragged to create the deposit; sometimes it seems that the palette knife or the brush has been flicked or flourished, documenting the gestural process.

In another parallel play within the installation, these quiet works also point toward something. As alluded to in their title, the paintings indicate the forces of gravity and direct us downward toward the core of the Earth. Like the *RELATIVE POINTS*, they employ material presence to situate us in the astrophysical.

# Material Testing

## Christine Corday and Lisa Le Feuvre in Conversation

LISA LE FEUVRE The erudition and complexity of your work demands questions that touch on expansive topics. It seems to me your creative processes are driven by an interrogation into how we insignificant and temporal humans try to make sense of both the world and the surrounding universe. You look to two measures to do this: science and the stars. These we like to think give us truth. I use my words carefully—we like to think they give us truth, but do they? The world is overwhelming, there is too much to know, and there is so much we will never understand. We try to fix our attention on something that appears to hold true: imponderables of time, space, and humanity call on methods of measurement, desires to find the limits.

CHRISTINE CORDAY The idea that humans in the cosmos are insignificant is the exact opposite of how I feel. The material truth of it is that we humans are, in fact, the scale of the cosmos.

LLF Tell me more.

CC The elements that are found within our bodies evolve through conditions of tremendous temperature and tremendous pressure in the stars. Or to say it another way, these elements are matter forged in the life and explosion of stars. These elements coalesce into yet more stars, planets, asteroids, and also become our bodies. When one looks from a material perspective, there is an incessant inseparability, connection, and meaning between humans and the cosmos. It is all relative. Take measurement as an example—measurement of one object means nothing without the measure of another in relation to it.

LLF Are you saying scale—that wonderful sculptural term—is what matters most? Scale is concerned with relationships, unlike size. It needs something that is not itself to operate.

CC Scale is very important because it brings no absolute frame of reference. My early work at NASA, where I worked on a SETI project (SETI standing for "Search for Extra-Terrestrial Intelligence," an important scientific research unit), informed a specific frame of reference. In this research-led project I set out to reduce the baseline of all known stars to a list of stars with axes either pole-on or perpendicular to our line of sight for use by our world's observatories when they set out to search for orbiting planets. Here, the scales of cosmology informed my perceptual bias. To my mind, I could never create anything truly

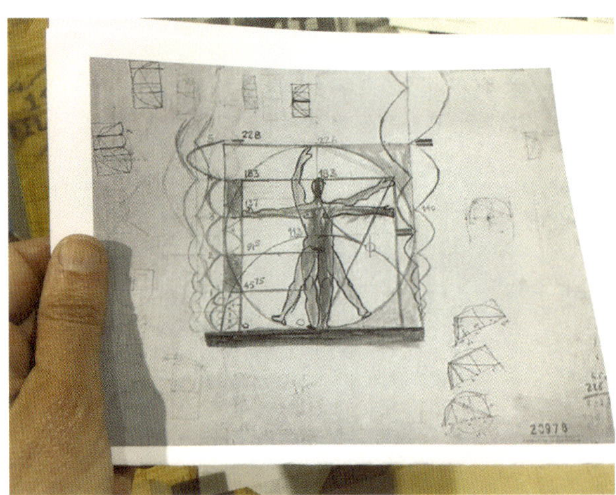

Le Corbusier, *Le Modulor* (Modulor Man), 1945, print-out in the artist's studio.

large on Earth: to really be large, any solid-state object I might make would need to exceed Earth while also sharing its surface.

LLF An impossibility.

CC Yes! Scale is not about limits of size, it refers to the fact that some objects are merely larger or smaller than others. When I consider the relativity of scale it brings me an opportunity to open the notion of an elemental signature, a shared architecture through the atomic structure of particle and fields. No matter the distance, or the material state, the element is always and exactly the same.

LLF How does this impact your sculpture?

CC So, when I am thinking of and making my sculpture, I perceive it as sharing an architecture of identity with the universe. This is a medium that I cannot touch in either a literal or atomic sense. But, having recognized this, I know my body contains it, as does the work I am making. Human understandings of scale have a history of using the body as a unit. The cubit, for example, is an ancient measure using the distance of elbow to forefinger, or there is Leonardo da Vinci's late-fifteenth-century Vitruvian Man, or Le Corbusier's mid-twentieth-century Modulor Man. These are beautiful ways of trying to understand the world. These examples construct relationships. Our perceptual system has been evolving over the last 600-million years. Just imagine the pace of that—and it still is not done, the human system is still evolving. Certain senses will no doubt fall away, others will develop. The human is a unit of witness that dissolves into awareness; we are all an aware medium, if you will. If you are looking out from your eyes, your fingertips, out of the cells of your body, you are doing this in relation to the cosmos—I mean this in a strictly material, not in a poetic, way. What I term human scale is materially present in science and the stars.

LLF Are you thinking of this scale as being objective? If yes, I agree—we all have bodies and we all measure ourselves in relation to our surroundings. But, at the same time, every single body is different. With your system, every scale is tailor-made to the perceiver.

CC Matter has a 13.8 billion-year provenance. I am interested in the elemental atoms—the smallest constituents of matter that identify as iron, as carbon . . . all of these things that are found within stars and within us. As we engage our evolving perceptual system, material measures itself. Human scale, in this understanding of it, is a scale of awareness of that fact. My system, yes, is a sliding scale, tailor-made as you say. This scale is one that extends or ends at the fingertips.

LLF Your words bring to mind that wise poem by Lucretius, *On the Nature of Things*, in which the Roman philosopher advises that “All nature, as it is in itself, consists of two things: there are bodies and there is a void in which these bodies are and through which they move.” Atom and void; void and atom. Both are relative and co-dependent. Are you saying that human beings are material, and that when we perceive, our material being is simply measuring other material?

CC Yes. If you want to open a measurement that includes this table in front of us that divides us as we speak, or if you want to open a measurement including us, the table, and the moon Ganymede, these relational points contain the same primary identities. They are simply in different phases, different molecular arrangements. There is a lot of seemingly empty space within the atom, as well as between matter itself. These voids fill with evolving understanding, and you need to choose where to pay attention.

LLF What are your thoughts on consensual forms of measurement—the meter, the inch, the mile, the kilometer? Metric is my first language, but imperial I can imagine with ease as it is based on the human body, something we all possess. It is always an act of translation. I move between the two systems depending on the context, but to shift from one to the other I need to imagine distance in relative terms. I am fascinated by the metric and imperial systems of measuring and how they differ. One is easy, because it builds up units of ten—easy mathematics. One is easy in a different way, because it relates to a body—the inch comes from the thumb. But not from my thumb—from a man's thumb—there it is subjective.

CC The measuring systems we use have inherent bias in them. Both humans and science seek to answer questions, build better tools, and come to certain conclusions that can be proved. Le Corbusier created the Modulor Man to combine the imperial with the metric into a new system of how to make things.

LLF Minimalism is an art historical moment that is one of your tools. What is it that fascinates you with it?

CC Much of my work comes from Minimalism. I am interested in reducing material to its medium, to its primary statement, to its raw signature that cannot be further reduced. My focus is on the elemental; that is my measuring stick. I started as a painter. There was a time when I could never imagine being a sculptor, or getting involved in form at all. However, I started making my own paint and it all changed. This made me go deeper and deeper into the medium of the medium. This brought me to structure, to an architecture that is completely elemental. When I was making paint I realized that I was not really manipulating the pigments, rather I was just suspending the elements in material states.

LLF And from here you moved to sculpture?

CC Yes. It occurred to me sculpture is no different. I was not manipulating the elements—the elemental metals—only suspending them in material states. The artist can form a line of sight straight into the medium of a work, into the medium-ness of the medium. It is then concerned with the material, a conversation that never steps outside of itself. Rothko often talked about how he considered himself a materialist, despite how exalted his work can be seen as being. Attention to material unlocks all of that—its most elegant, furthest reduced form.

LLF You came to sculpture by taking account of the body, and through a human action—making paint. The moment you take account of the body you have

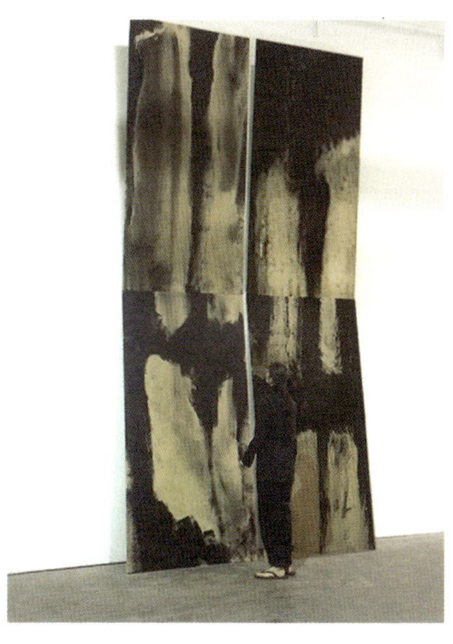

Christine Corday
*PERCES POLYPTYCH*
2016
Loose charcoal, synthetic polymer, and pigment on wood
192 × 97 × 1 in.
Photo: Corday Studio

relativity between different bodies (human and otherwise) in space—you feel scale. What I love about sculpture is the palpable, physical, mobile, and phenomenological experience it demands. It must be experienced in the present tense. I like to argue at any opportunity that sculpture is the most democratic artform. We make objects to make sense of the world, and just when we think we understand it an unexpected object gets in the way. Sculpture is all about objects and space, relationships, and material.

CC My first encounter with the object was the object as instrument—literally. It was the piano, which informs much of my subsequent work. The piano is an object that allows hands to trace the movement of a composer's choices—all pianos and all pianists join at its notes. A composition is a shared space. In a manner this is similar to the elements in the periodic table, the very same keys are shared by all who sit at it—ideas collect, overlap, share, repeat. That is its democracy. Had I started off with the violin, or the cello or the flute, or some kind of percussion it may have led me somewhere else. The body of the piano is always greater in measurement relative to the person who sits at it. At the piano you have absolute awareness of the instrument, and one's presence with it makes a difference. The sensation or learning from touch, too, is important with sculpture—complete perceptual awareness.

LLF When you are talking about perception, are you just talking about looking and listening?

CC No—all the senses. Touch is the contact of the skin—the largest sensory organ—with something else. I think of touch in terms of sensation and seeing. In the literal sense, touch is a sensation hovering or suspended at an unfathomably small distance from the object. As sculptor I am interested in how medium can exceed the object. There are billions of stimuli occurring right now as we are talking. There have been so many studies of the vast and still unknown aspects of perception, raising so many questions. If one sense is impaired, what happens to the others? How do senses evolve? What is a sensory experience and what is a pre-determined response from our brain? To sense involves all of the senses.

LLF We are always editing as we perceive—it is fascinating how we can turn off perception. We are sitting in a bar talking right now where there are other conversations, where ice is being prepared for the upcoming cocktail hour, there are visual distractions. Yet it is possible to decide where to perceive, to put on blinkers to control attention. John Cage advised "the world changes according to the place we place our attention. This process is addictive and energetic." Language cannot exist without the spaces between the words. These silences—that can be short, long, protracted, uncomfortable, portentous, all depending on the context—are what enables language to exist, be it textual, aural, or visual. It is another form of relativity.

CC That contact point for perception is about a quality, not a quantity.

LLF When do you know when a work is finished? When do you know when to stop?

CC First there is the idea, then the physical form.

LLF So tell me first about the idea.

CC When to stop with the idea? Well there is working as an artist in the exalted sense, and working as an artist in the professional sense. I once wondered if Beethoven or Mozart heard their entire symphonies all at once, or say the violin only. When to stop with the making? In painting, it is an immediate sense—the painter walks away the minute the artwork has life of its own. Even if I feel, or I

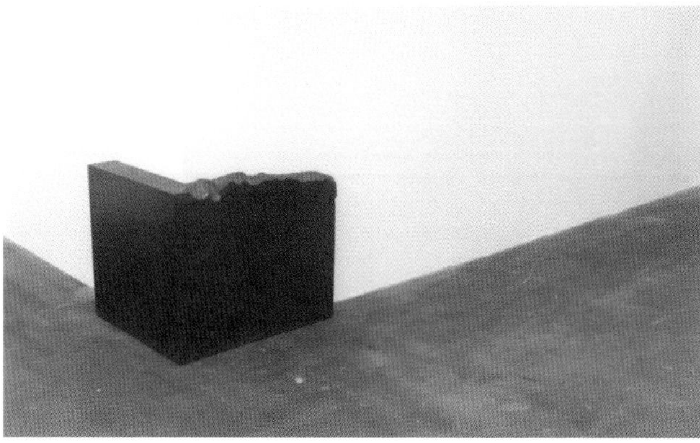

Christine Corday
*AHN*
2009
Carbon steel
24 × 56 × 4½ in.
Photo: Enrico Gomez

should say felt, as I no longer paint, a painting needs one more strike of yellow, I must not follow through. It might torture me, but the painting is complete. The painting has left my hands. With sculpture it is a little different, especially when you are getting into objects that are heavily fabricated and handled by many people. That is a different story. That gets down to details. Unintentional things may happen, and you may leave those, or you may edit out others. The sculpture, too, slowly makes its way.

LLF I think of your current works as both sculptures and as events, each object has a temporal quality and has been brought into being through a series of material events. When the sculpture is complete you release them out of your control, and they live in the world—they work on and are worked on by all that surrounds them.

CC In the *Protoist* series the moment before melt becomes cut is a material state between liquid and solid, and a window between phases of materiality. "Protoist" is a term I created to describe form in and out of a solid state. This is a series of works that live somewhere in the suspension of a moment between sensory perception and its definition. These sculptures focus on temperature, solid states of elemental metal, and the sensory effect of touch with abstract form.

LLF Let's return to the piano—a form that is brought into form through the fingers and through the ears. The volume—again, that very sculptural term—comes out of this object.

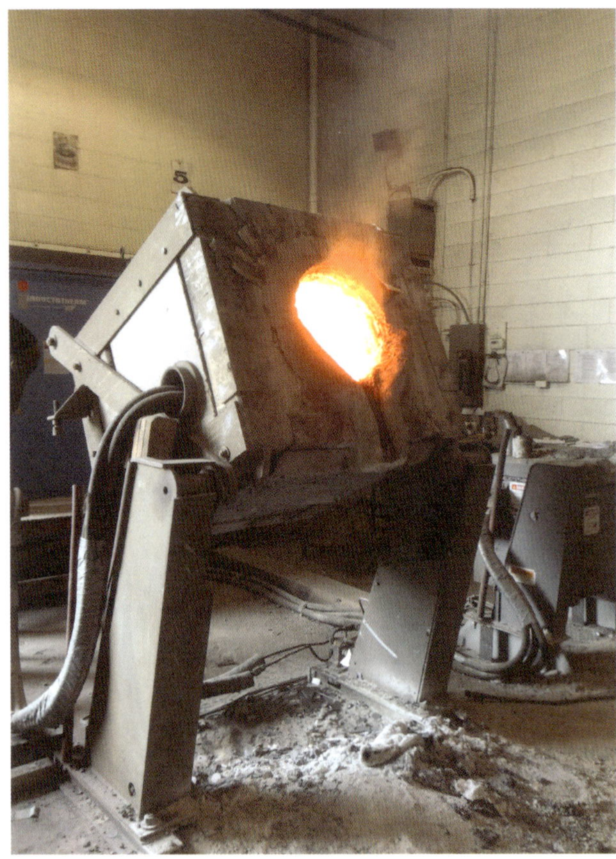

Foundry furnace used in the fabrication of *KNOUN*, 2016, Bernier Cast Metals, Michigan.

CC I wonder what would Beethoven be without the invention of the pianoforte? The two are intertwined, just as art and science are intertwined. I am interested in the moment of finding the instrument of expression. I think it is the architect Louis Kahn who says "hammering away at the door of the sun, demanding an instrument of expression for nobility, love, hate"—I don't know the exact words, but you get the sense. I pinned these words up in my Brooklyn studio—for me the phrase is very Beethoven, not at all Mozart. I can see Beethoven hammering away, and how the pianoforte had to come to be. The artist's tools are exquisite and exact, and then evolve in the studio. My tools are informed by the hammer and the chisel on the cosmological scale. I am interested in the fundamental forces, just as much in how our planet formed as in my next sculpture is forming. When the Earth was being pummeled, all of that heat, that turning over of material that is no different from what we experience when in the foundry, the forge, or with nuclear fusion tokamaks and tools of stars. . . . It is reiterating material becoming.

LLF At the moment I am reading Elizabeth Grosz's thoughts on why art matters. In her 2008 book *Chaos, Territory, Art: Deleuze and the Framing of the Earth* she says—and I love her words so much that they are blazed into my brain: "Art is intensely political not in the sense that it is a collective or community activity (which it may be but usually is not) but in the sense that it elaborates the possibilities of new, more different sensations than those we know." She argues art comes in advance of articulation, that its productive power can harness what is felt but yet to be framed by words. Like Samuel Beckett, she warns art should not be concerned with self-expression. Art is a generative and intellectual discipline that raises necessary and urgent questions for the present. As Grosz describes it: "sensations, or artworks, do not signify or represent [. . .] they assemble, they make, they do, they produce." An art that matters is an art that anticipates what is to come, that harnesses burgeoning ideas still to be settled into language. The purpose of art is not to provide beautiful relief from an unfathomable world, rather it is to address imponderables, to make the world yet more complicated. Art has the ability to create a force with which questions can be raised and problems opened. I want to wrestle with the idea of expression—Beckett and Grosz are interested in what the art does, what sensations it brings forth, not in what it expresses.

CC For me it is the material that is the expression, the material that is informed by forces, by laws of nature. I do not see art as a form of personal expression, that is not how I come about the work. Like Philip Glass's arpeggios. They are not about his personage. The arpeggio is a minimalist tool; its repetition is reductive and reveals a certain mark within the material—within the sound. It is about . . . a certain becoming. I know this is a word I often use, but it does not matter which verb you use. It is just word-play, I think it is the tone of the verb that matters. For me it is about opening up the definition of the human as the material, meaning that self-expression is just another form of material-becoming. What matters to me is standing from a point of awareness at a material level. To me that is all sculpture. The human aspect is what is fascinating, the human material aspect.

LLF Word-play and sculpture of course brings us to Richard Serra's list of verbs from 1967 and to Bruce Nauman's lexicon in his 2004 *Raw Materials*, and tone brings us back to music. It seems that you are really interested in an amorphous sculptural quality of material.

CC Yes, what is changeless within change in form is my medium. This is what I want to work with and how I see as a sculptor.

LLF I want to hear more about your use of collaboration—you always work with others. How does the work of the work interest you? The teams who you work with are like atoms in constant motion until the work is complete.

CC You know, metals, too, work in teams. Different from all other elements, metals atomically share their electrons, effectively they give up all their electrons among the group. The metallic bond keeps the strength of its structure from this freeing all the electrons—there is collaboration even within the material.

LLF We are talking today on the occasion of a forthcoming exhibition. Can you share in advance how you are thinking of choreographing the works together in space? Minimalism I know is important to you, and when the medium is pared back all the conditions of display speak loudly. Once this conversation is published it will of course be fascinating to see the gap between the imagined projection and the reality. Your incredibly acute perception of elements in space means each decision will be taken with great care. For you an exhibition is a moment of, to steal from the philosopher of science Karl Popper, expanding beyond the limits of your known horizon.

CC I would love it if the exhibition might provoke people to momentarily lift a definition of center and reposition their perception somewhere else. We are entering into the fourth Copernican Revolution. The first is the fact that the Earth is not the center of the heavens—before this we thought the sun revolved around the Earth. To move from this orientation was to understand the heretical fact that the Earth moved around the sun. The second was that the sun was not center of the heavens either, nor our solar system. The third development was to understand that the Milky Way—and this was a recent as the 1940s, '50s, and '60s—was not at the center of the universe, and that it is one of trillions of galaxies in this universe. And now we are realizing that to understand the nature of space time we need to realize that there is no center, meaning that center is everywhere. In this exhibition, each one of the forms on display points everywhere and nowhere. Each form is made up of ten-thousand pounds of iron points and my exploration is to find comfort in replacing center with everywhere or nowhere.

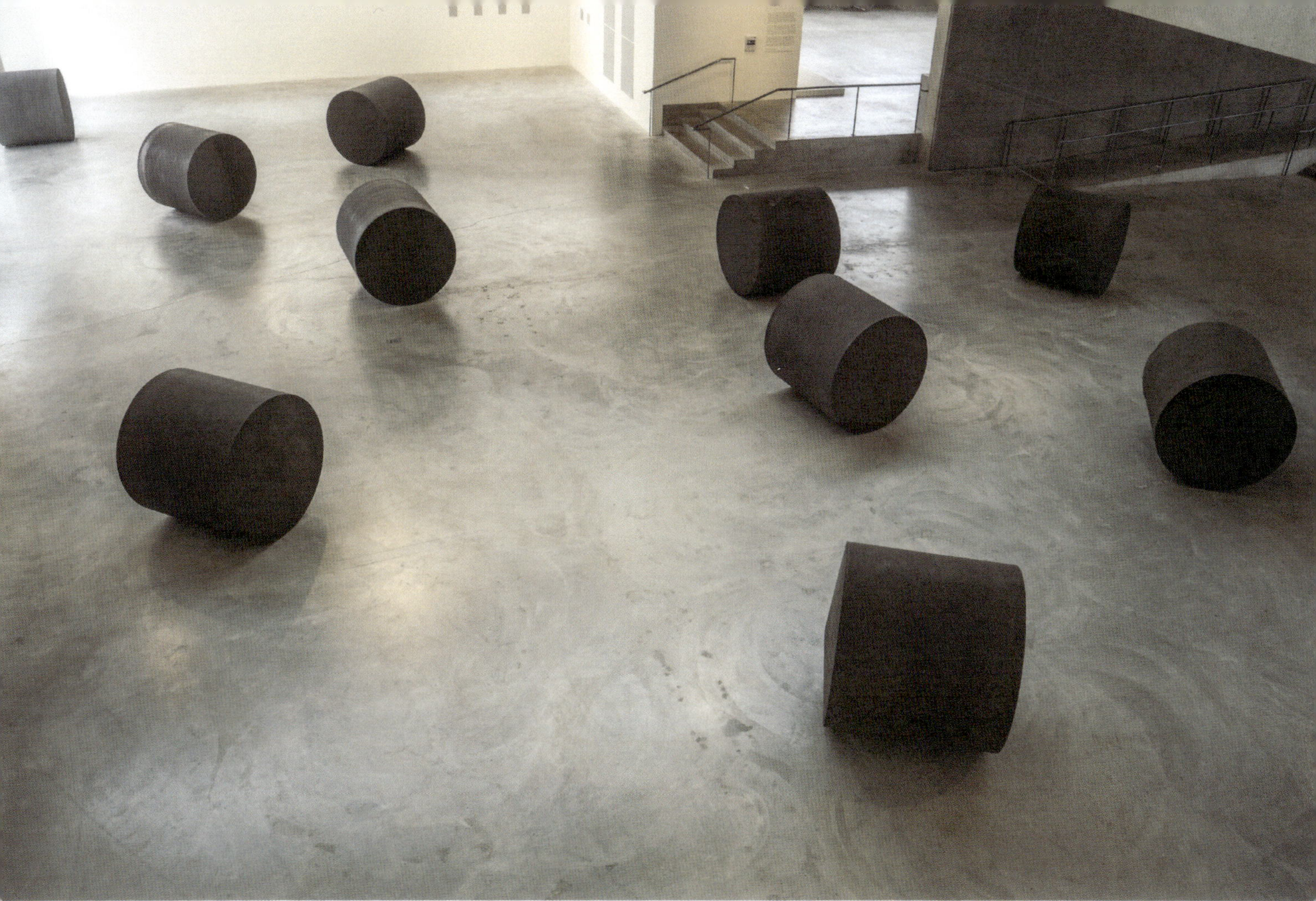

*Christine Corday.*
*RELATIVE POINTS*, installation view, Contemporary Art Museum St. Louis, January 18–April 21, 2019. Photo: Dusty Kessler

LLF Do you embrace failure in your work? To think of failure in productive terms can open new ideas—of course we must always be wary of who can fail. In science, failure is not a judgment, it is a fact of research. By failing we can learn limits and possibilities—we are terrified of failure, but we all know it better than we care to admit.

CC I suppose there is a sliding scale as well to failure. Ideas, I think, never fail. But then the execution is a sliding scale of failure. I deal with failure on a daily basis . . .

LLF . . . so I guess that means you are human. It is these porous boundaries of perception and understanding that can bring about new knowledge, and new (or if not new, alternative) ways of understanding our place in the world.

November 5, 2018

# The Point of Relativity

Michael Govan

Christine Corday's large-scale metal sculptures are reminiscent of work from a previous generation of Minimalist artists that she admires. Raw metal abstractions of imposing size and weight with intentional geometries, her work is often made on an architectonic scale for public spaces and large galleries, not for an art collector's living room. And like sculptor Richard Serra, Corday is fascinated by testing the physical limits of manipulating metal under heat and pressure and is interested in how large sculpture always has a relationship to our body and our movement. But that's where the similarity ends.

Corday's sculptures address an entirely different set of concerns about materiality. At the most intimate scale, Corday usually encourages us to touch her work, connecting not just our eyes, but the sensory organ of our skin to help make sense of her enigmatic constructions. I can image this impulse in her work as an extension of her classical training to play piano, where art is made through touch. At the other infinite extreme, Corday aligns her compositions to the scale of the cosmos, somehow always connected to the out-there. She constantly reminds us that we, and the eyes and skin with which we might perceive her sculpture, are made of stardust. There's no real difference between the materiality of the cosmos and ourselves. Materiality is all shared and connected like the electrons shared between the atoms in the chemical bonds that make her metal strong. I suppose that's a natural thing to think about when your college astronomy research got you working with NASA before becoming an artist, as Corday did.

Corday's sculptures aren't about expressing herself through form. Rather she shapes and constructs material to tease us, through our experience and thought, into feeling our own sense of being—to feel our own personal, intimate materiality through touch, as well as to feel our real immediate connectedness to the whole of the cosmos. It's an ambitious project indeed!

Corday blends an intense artistic and scientific sense of inquiry. She is still developing her practice through focused research and experimentation and is making artistic breakthroughs in each of her usually monumental new projects.

Through her new work in St. Louis, Corday takes us into a new territory of experience, pushing materiality into immateriality. Not a singular sculptural form but rather many (twelve) forms of similar shape and volume situated in diverse orientations across the interior of a large gallery, her *RELATIVE POINTS* installation literally points us in many directions at once.

Each form is a kind of cylinder on its side, one end flat, and one end made with a very shallow cone so that each form appears to "point" in a direction. The directions seem random and each feels tentatively placed and as if with some force they could be rolled or point in another direction. I remember from grade school that little bits of iron will point toward a magnetic field, and these sculptures are made of bits of metal, even if collected into a weighty whole that I can't quite imagine moving without substantial force.

Rather than using heat to chemically bond metals into a singular alloy, the objects that comprise *RELATIVE POINTS* are formed through compression. In each, a massive 10,000 pounds of tiny bits of elemental metal and metalloid grit are forced together into a shape under enormous pressure. They appear solid and singular, but in fact are quite different from the metal cousins of Corday's other sculptures. Each of these substantial "points" retains a quality of the multiplicity of their nearly countless constituent points of material. And as a whole the weighty large forms are a concentration of energy pointing in a multiplicity of directions.

As the artist herself describes, and it seems quite evident wandering through her installation, there is no center and no order of direction—as in our universe. Centuries ago humans were shocked to learn that we, or even our planet, aren't the center of anything, and increasingly so as we discover how truly immense, diverse, uncentered, and ever-expanding our universe is. To bring that back to the locality of our own skin, one can't help but think about the many directions in which we point, and how relative direction can be if we imagine ourselves, as in fact we are, in the midst of a decentered cosmos. The real substance of Corday's multipart sculpture is not its materiality but rather the enormous immaterial space between each element and the points in distant or infinite space implied by their directionality.

So much relativity, so many directions, and everything decentered—is that disorder? Or is it, as perhaps Corday suggests to me in her newest work, the true relative order that connects everything?

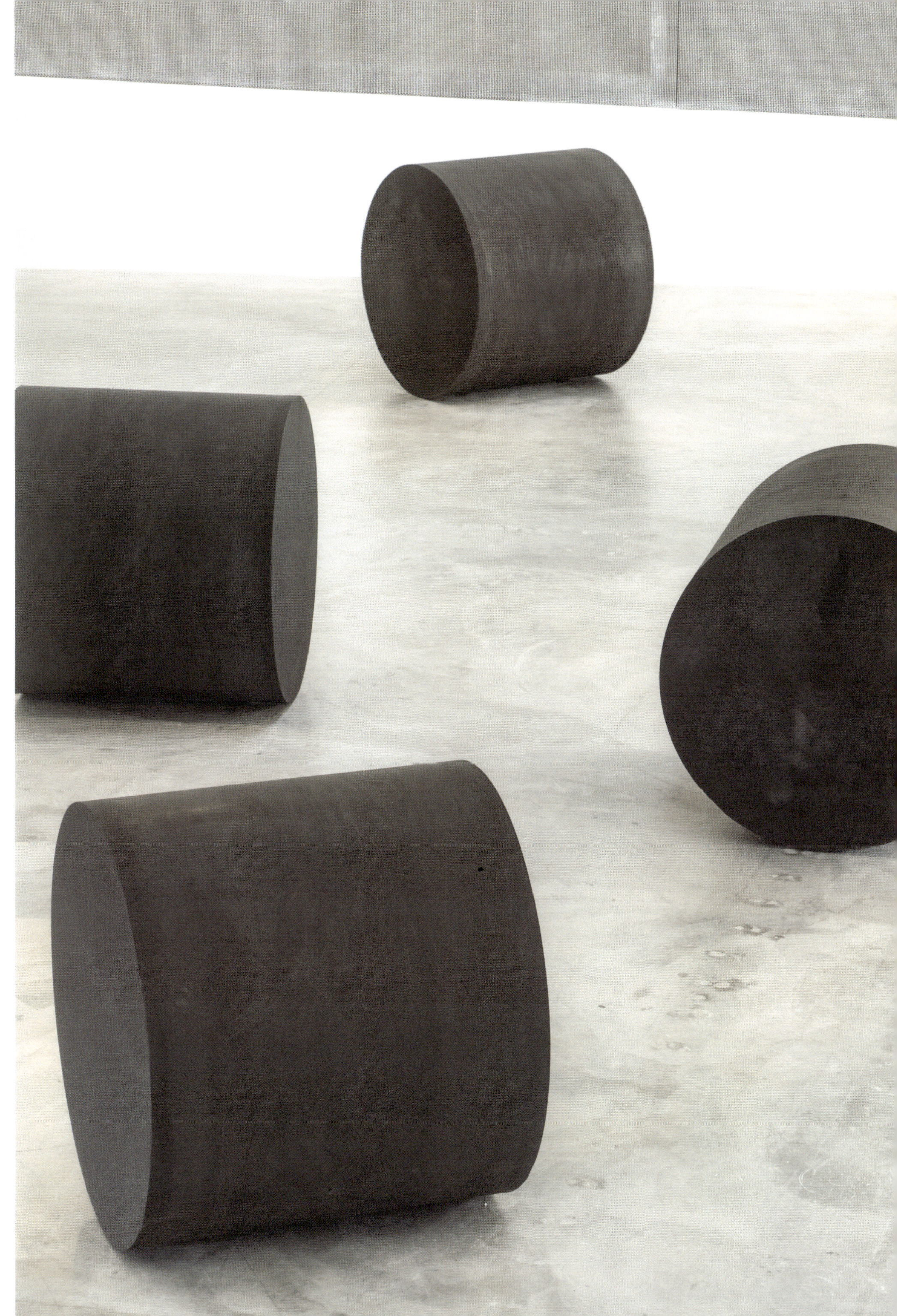

# Past Works

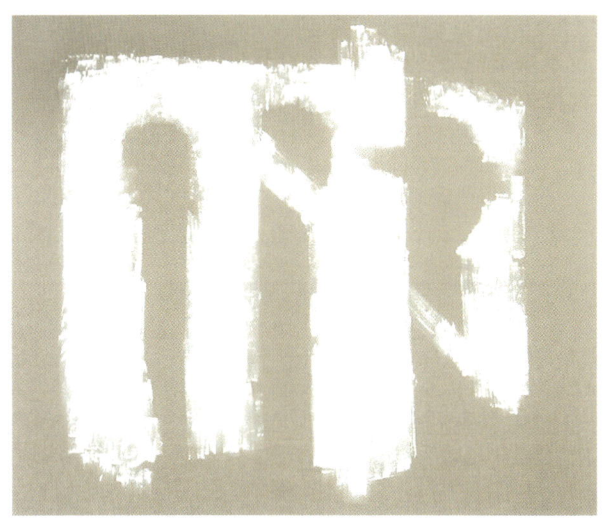

Christine Corday
*HELDAN III*
2008
Synthetic polymer and pigment on raw linen
94 × 119 in.
Collection of Alexandria and Peter Gordon Strelow
Photo: Michael Gold

Christine Corday
*PROME*
2006
Synthetic polymer and pigment on raw linen
63 × 111 in.
Collection of SOM Architects, San Francisco
As Overseen by Partner Craig W. Hartman
Photo: Michael Gold

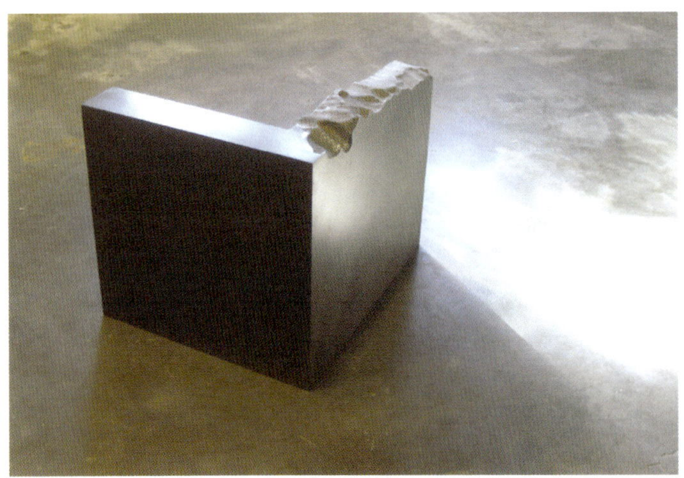

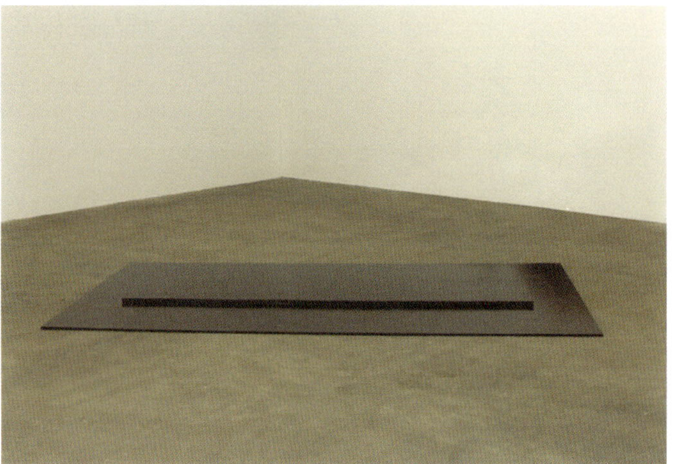

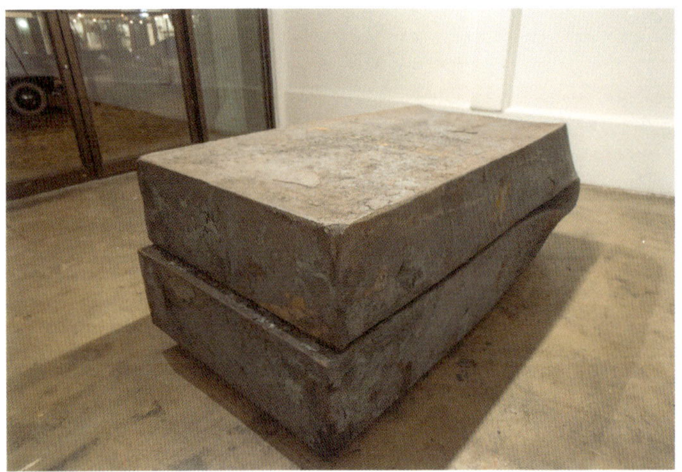

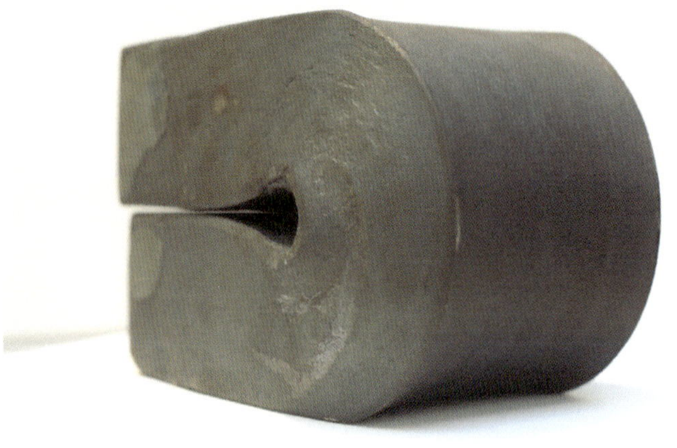

Christine Corday
*AHN*
2009
Carbon steel
24 × 56 × 4½ in.
Photo: Corday Studio

Christine Corday
*+2150F 6500000p*
2017
Elemental metal
20 × 63 × 30 in.
Photo: Jessica Baran

Christine Corday
*ÆPI*
2010
Pigment-coated aluminum
60 × 120 × 1½ in.
Photo: Daniel Terra

Christine Corday
*+2000F 9090p*
2017
Elemental metal
6 × 5½ × 8½ in.
Photo: Jessica Baran

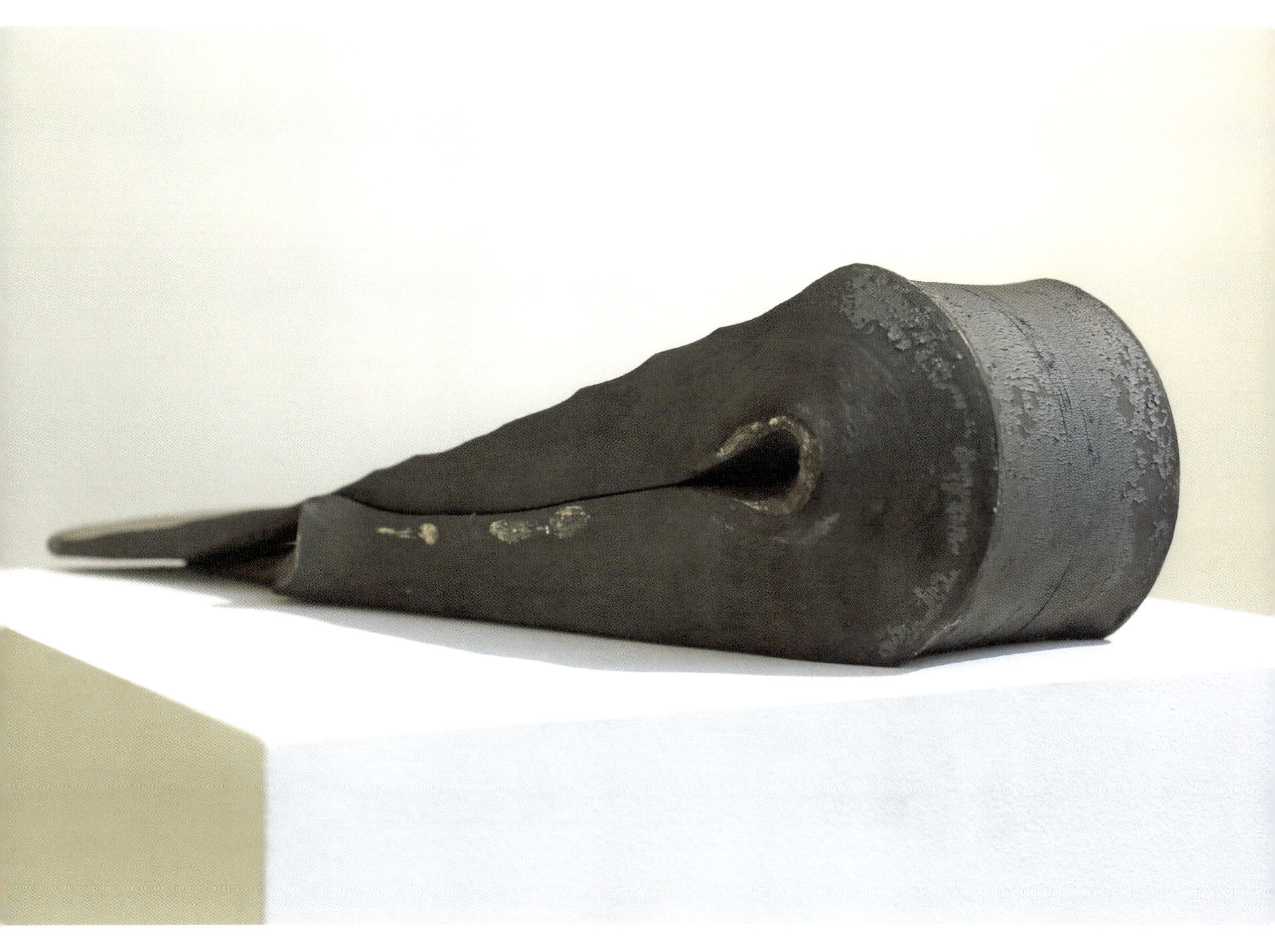

Christine Corday
*+2000F 28571p*
2017
Elemental metal
6 × 5½ × 15 in.
Photo: Jessica Baran

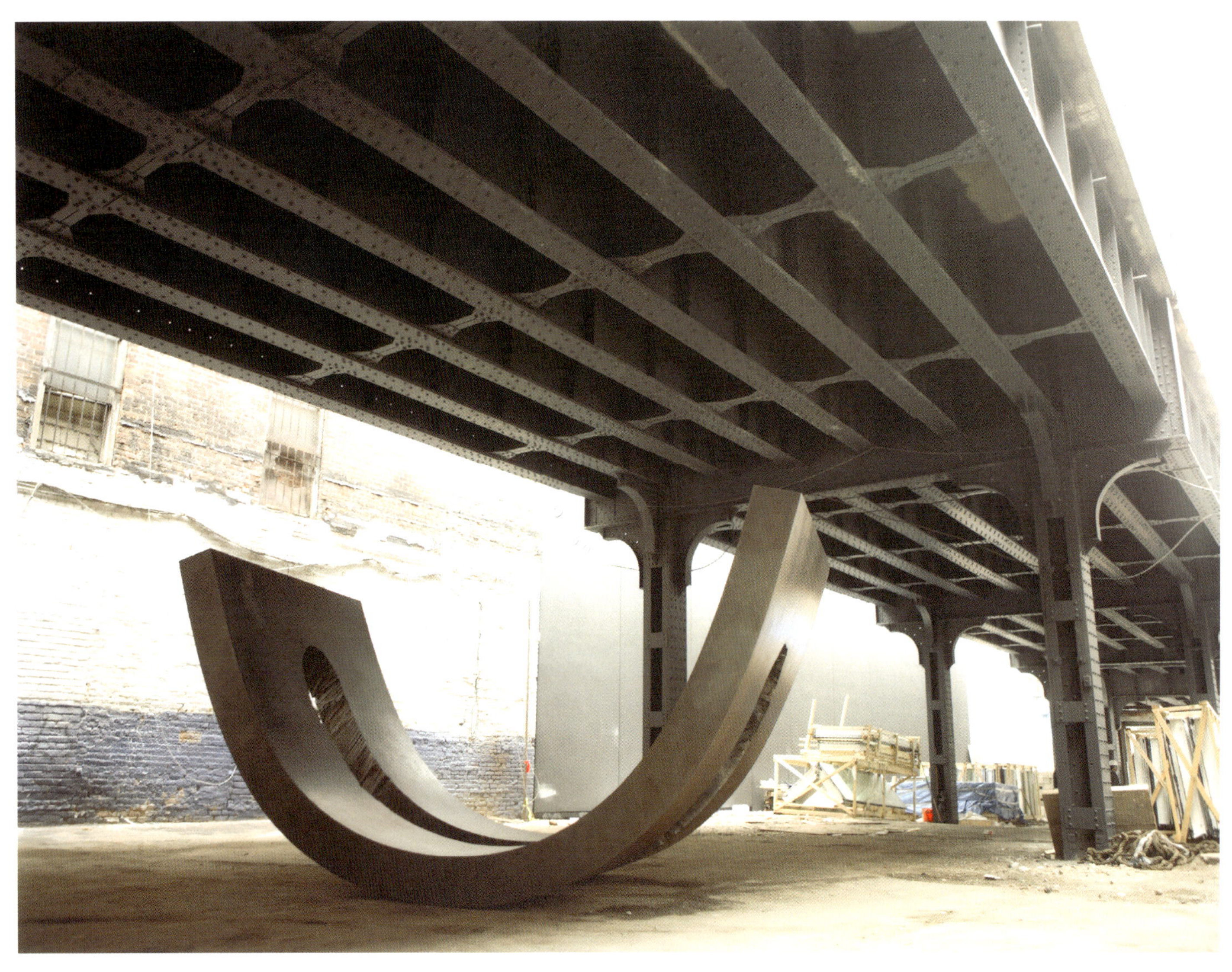

Christine Corday
*UNE*, installation view, High Line,
New York
2008
Weathering steel
105 × 103 × 197 in.
Photo: Tim Willis Lockbox Productions,
2008

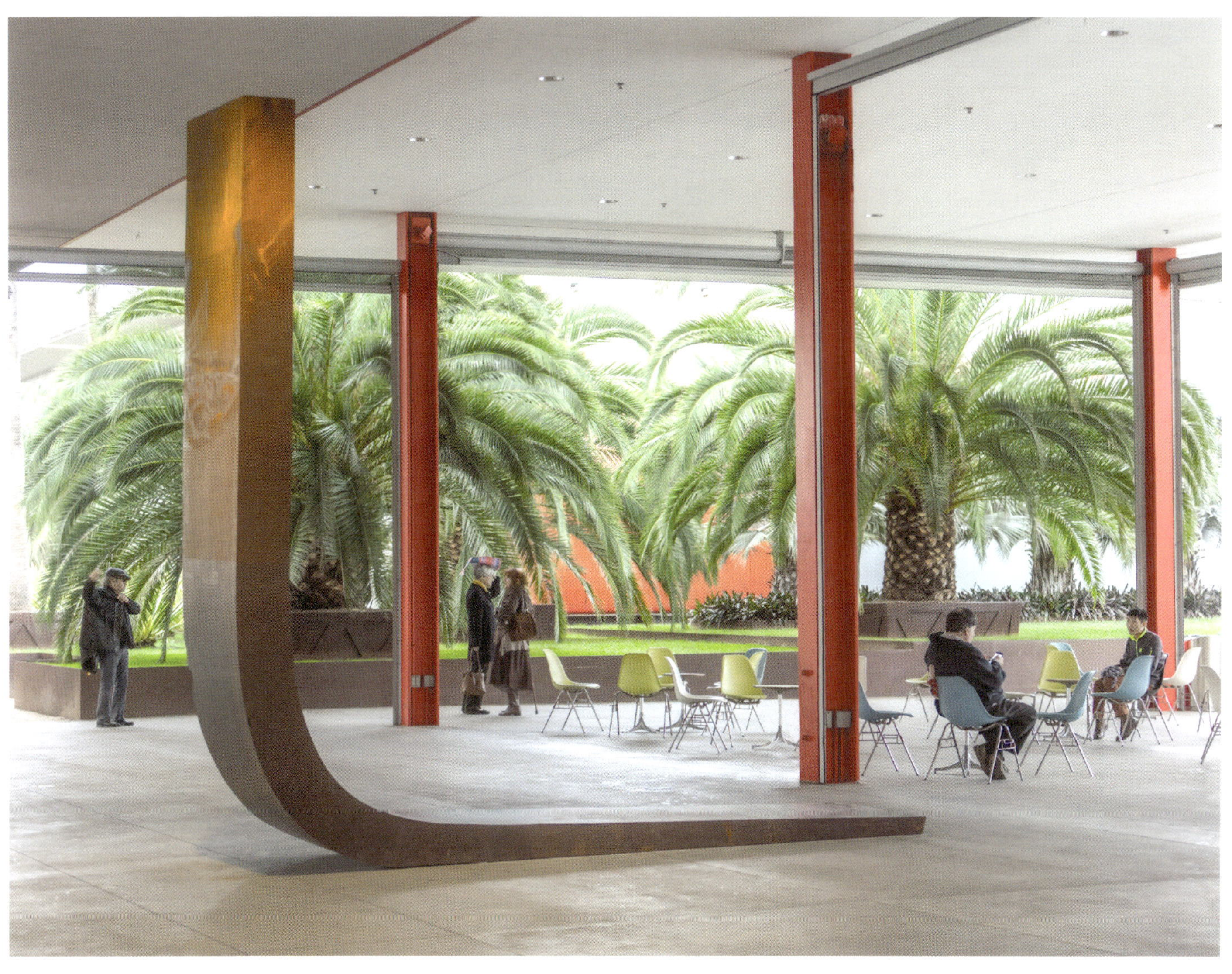

Christine Corday
*KNOUN*, installation view, *Christine Corday: Protoist Series, Selected Forms*,
Los Angeles County Museum of Art,
December 13, 2014–April 5, 2015
2014
Weathering alloy steel
156 × 150 × 40 in.

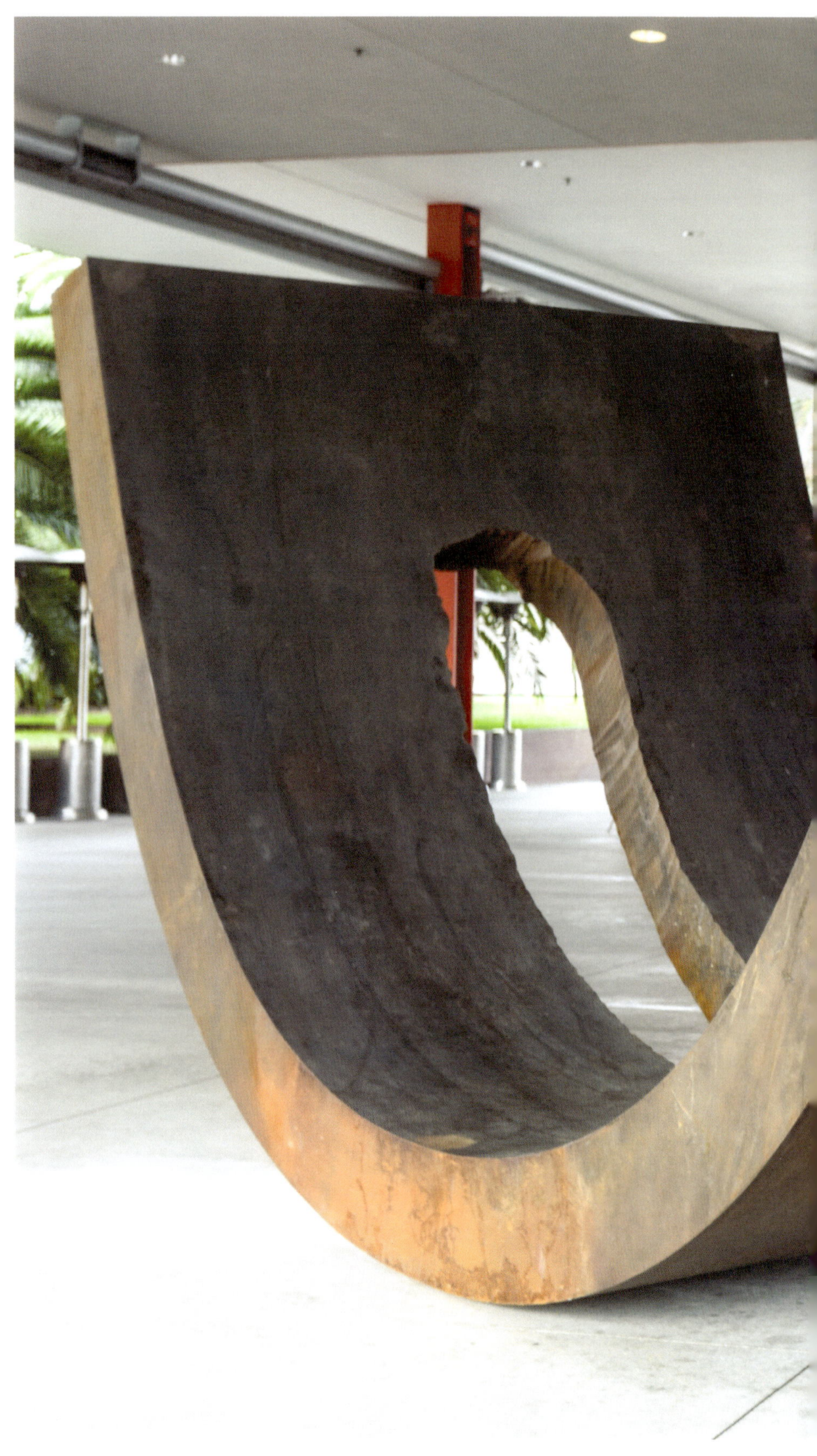

Christine Corday
*UNE*, installation view,
*Christine Corday: Protoist Series, Selected Forms*,
Los Angeles County Museum of Art, December 13, 2014–April 5, 2015
Weathering steel
105 × 103 × 197 in.
Photo © Museum Associates/ LACMA

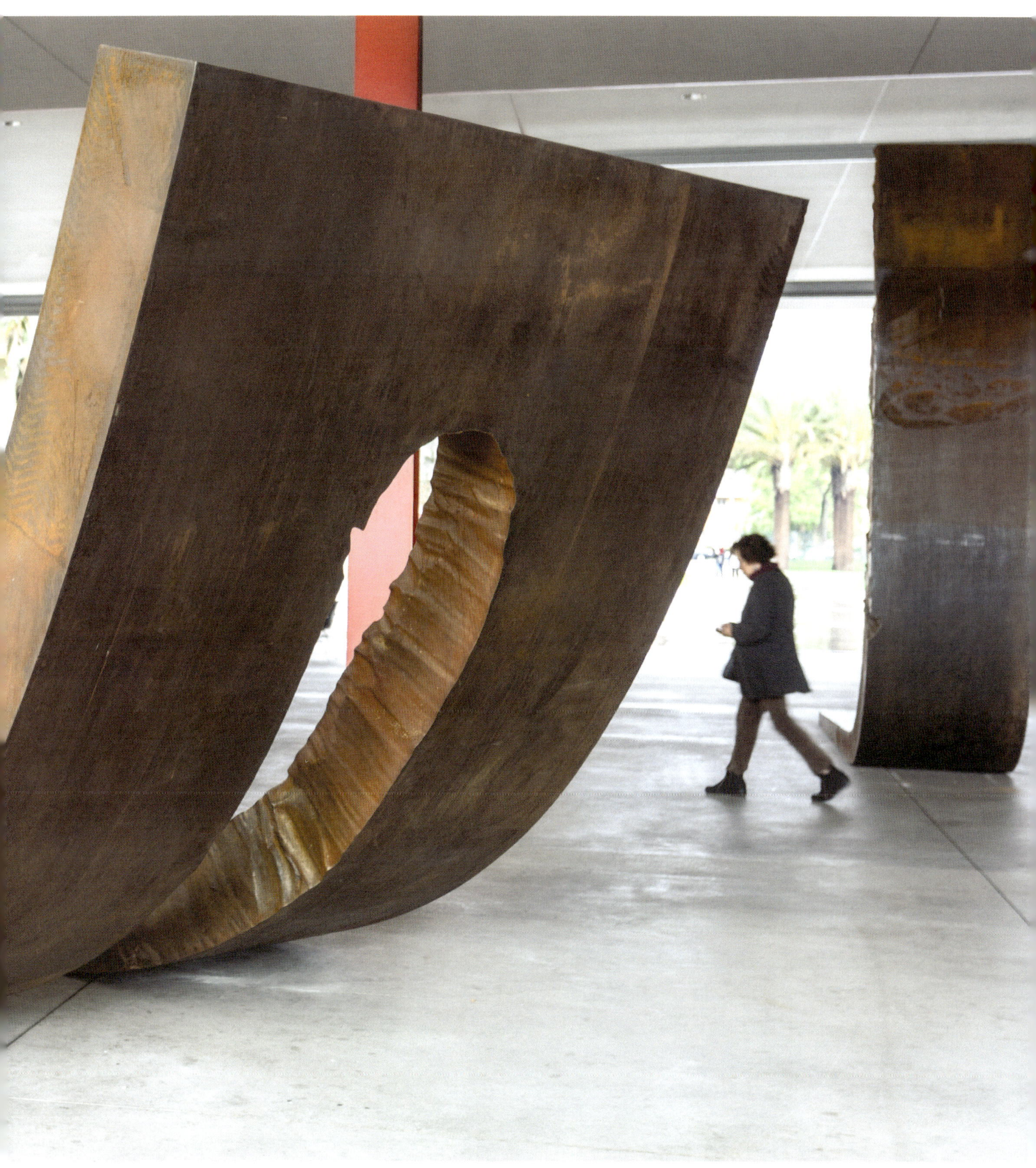

Process

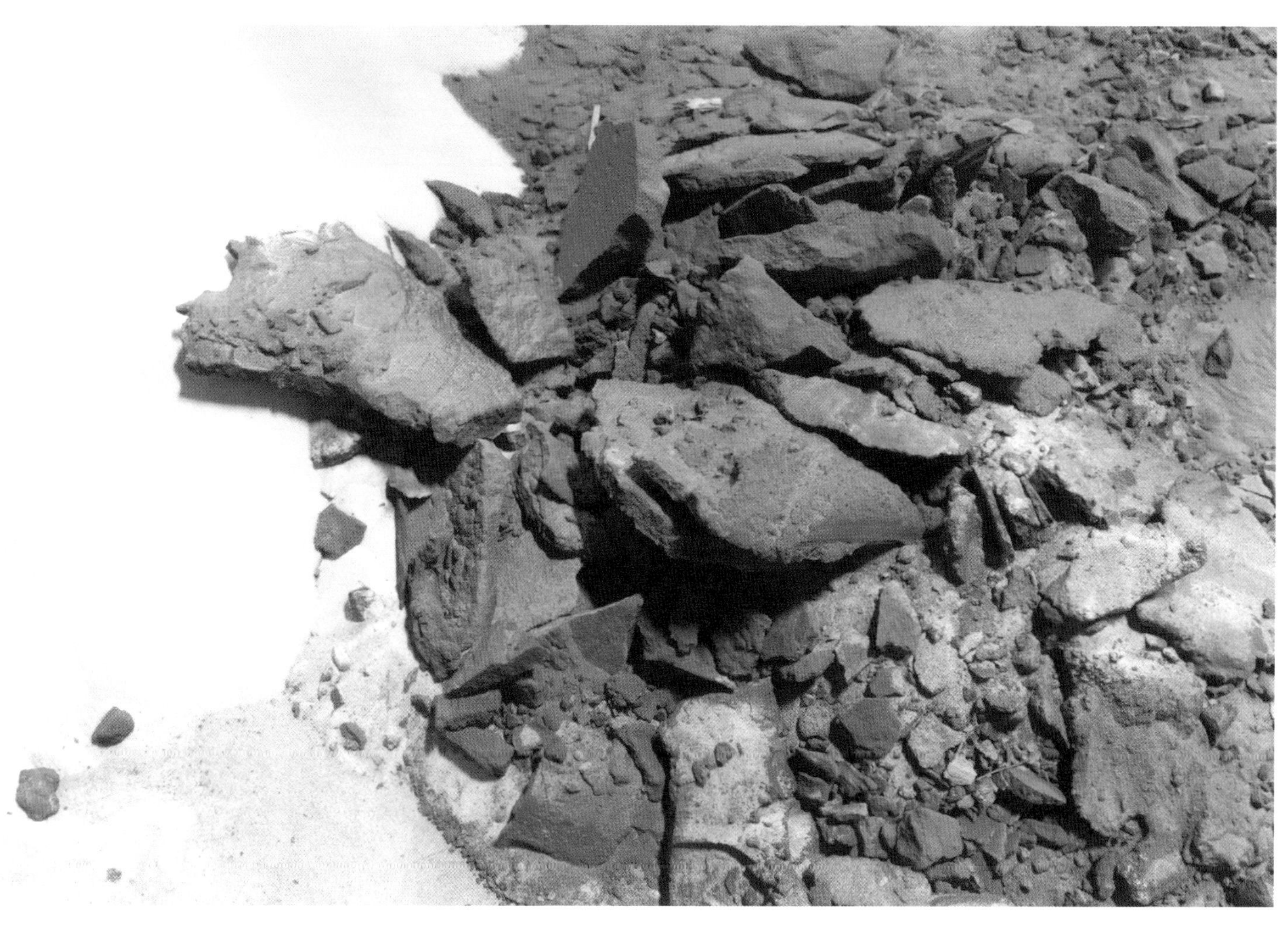

Iron grit used in *RELATIVE POINTS* production at Palmer Manufacturing and Supply, Ohio.

RELATIVE POINTS//CAMstl/
CORDAY/

MULTIPLE MONUMENTAL INSTALLATION / LOCATIONS RELATIVE TO CAMSTL / OTHER SAINT LOUIS POSSIBLE

1. *Under Cantilever, with point 1/4" from concrete side of museum*
2. *Under Cantilever, with point at edge of light concrete meeting sidewalk*
3. *On broken concrete slab at Spring and Olive*

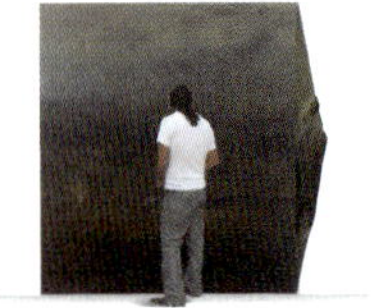

SIDE VIEW

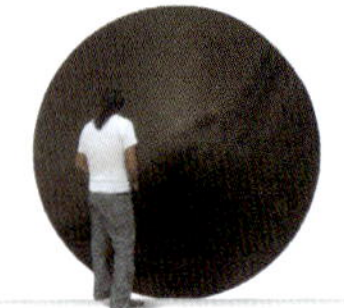

CONICAL TIP
FACE-ON

MONUMENTAL
RELATIVE POINTS

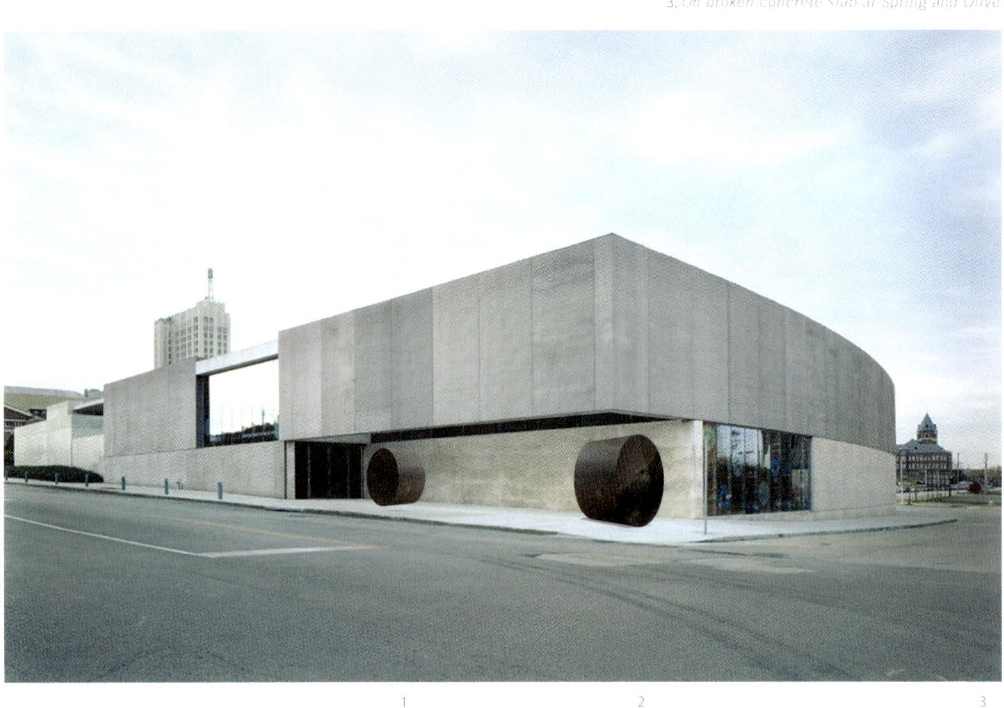

1 2 3

Artist proposal for *RELATIVE POINTS*, possible scale and placement, November 2015.

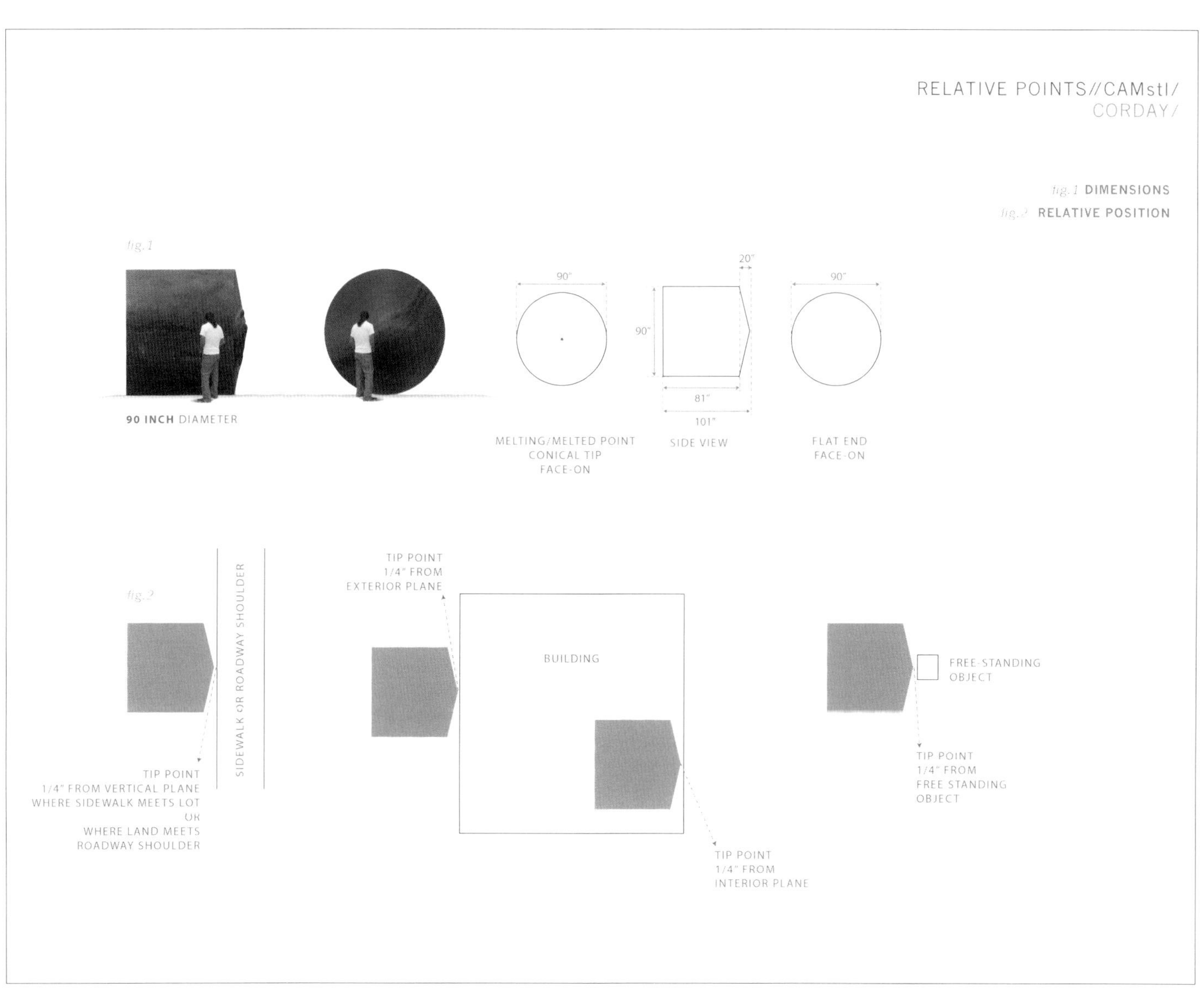


Artist drawings and schematics for *RELATIVE POINTS*, November 2015.

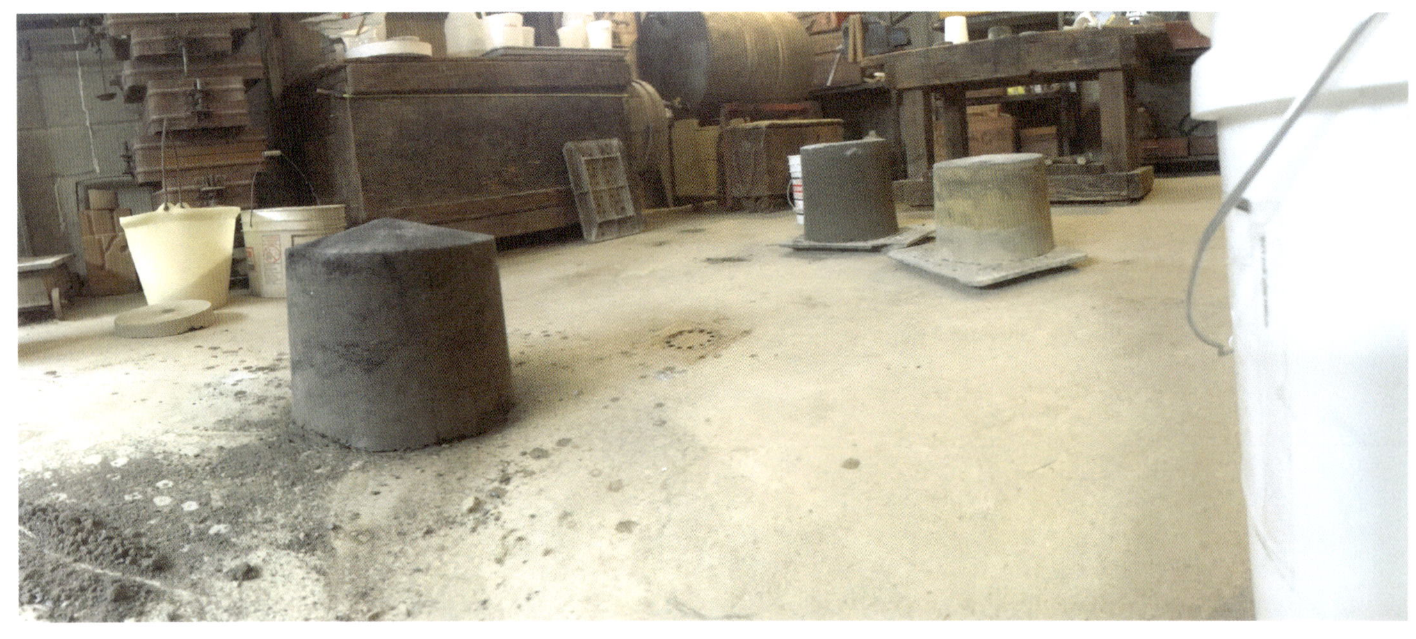

*RELATIVE POINT* prototypes, including cast in ferrosilicon and black iron oxide; ferrosilicon, silicon, black iron oxide, and iron grit; silicon and black iron oxide; in Paul Henry McMahill Studio, New York, February 2018.

(opposite)
Corday with *RELATIVE POINT* mold in her New York studio, January 2018.

(following spreads)
*RELATIVE POINTS* in production at Palmer Manufacturing and Supply, Ohio, December 2018 / January 2019.

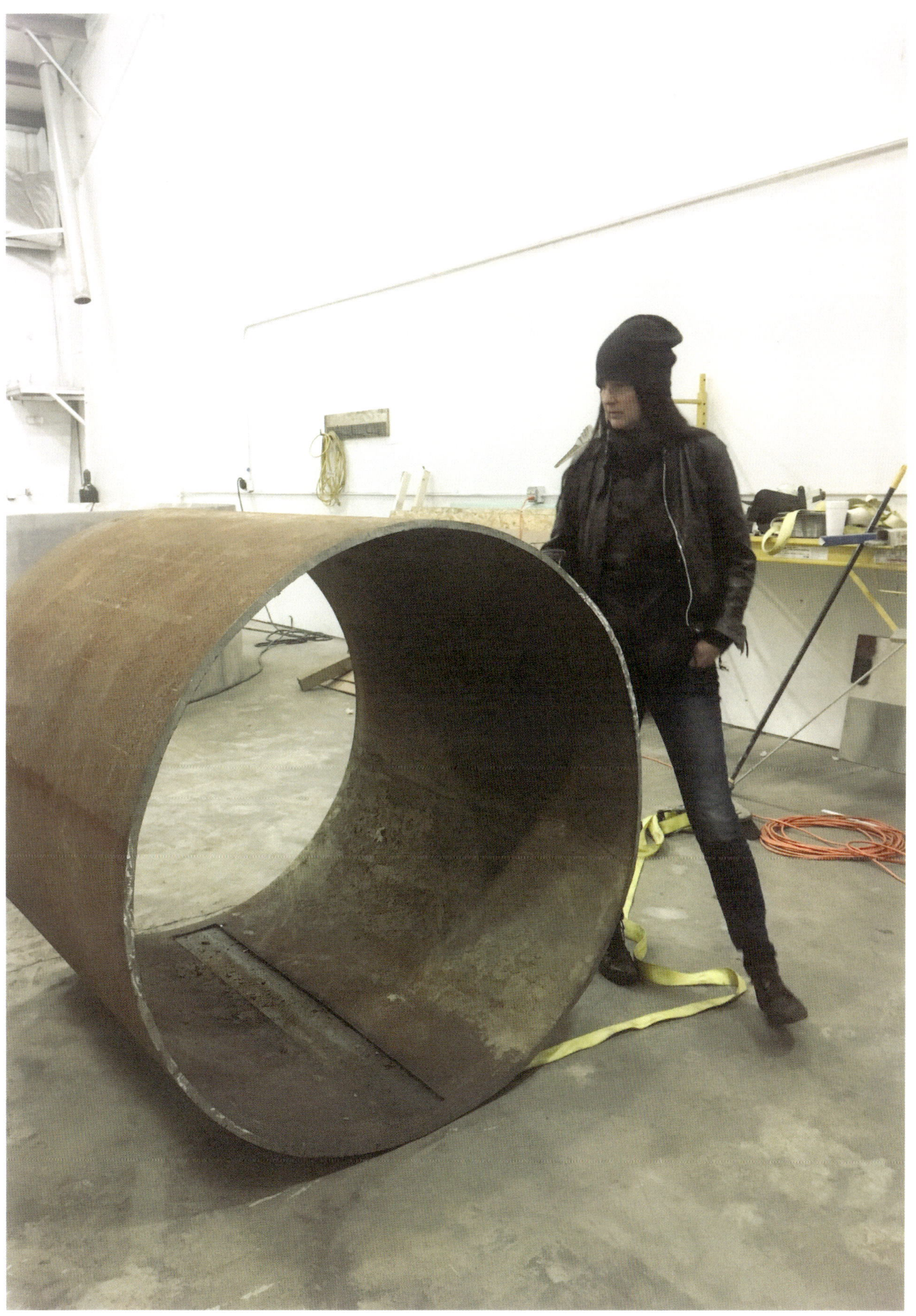

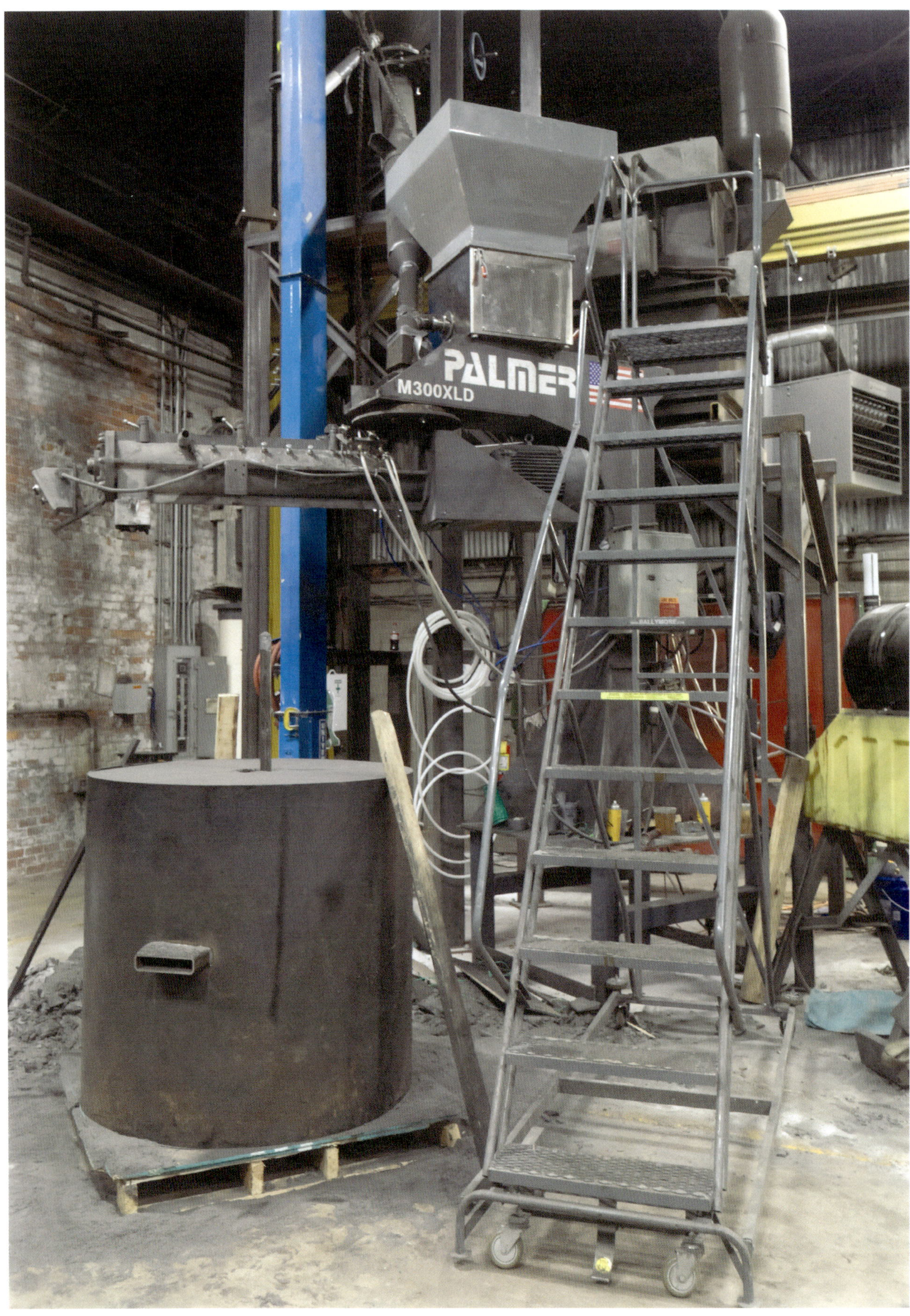
PALMER
M300XLD

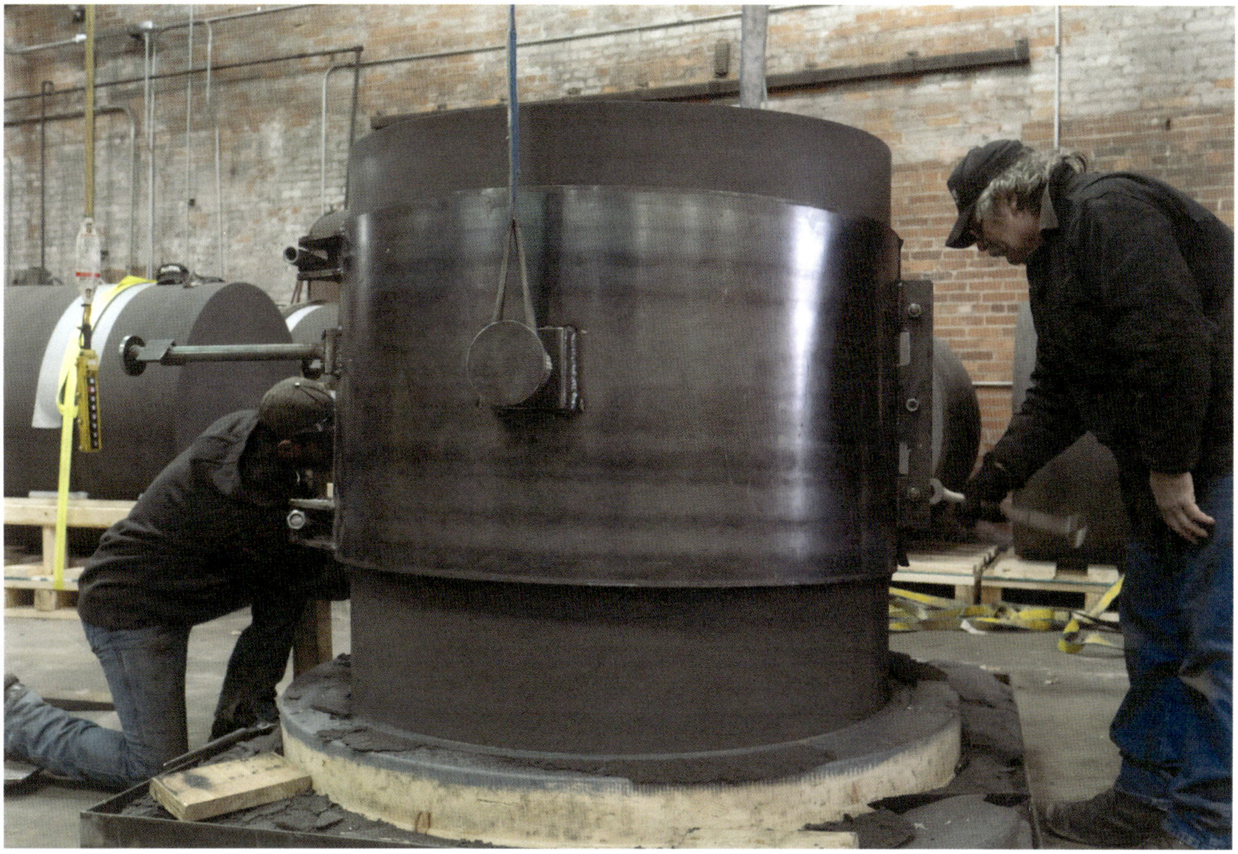

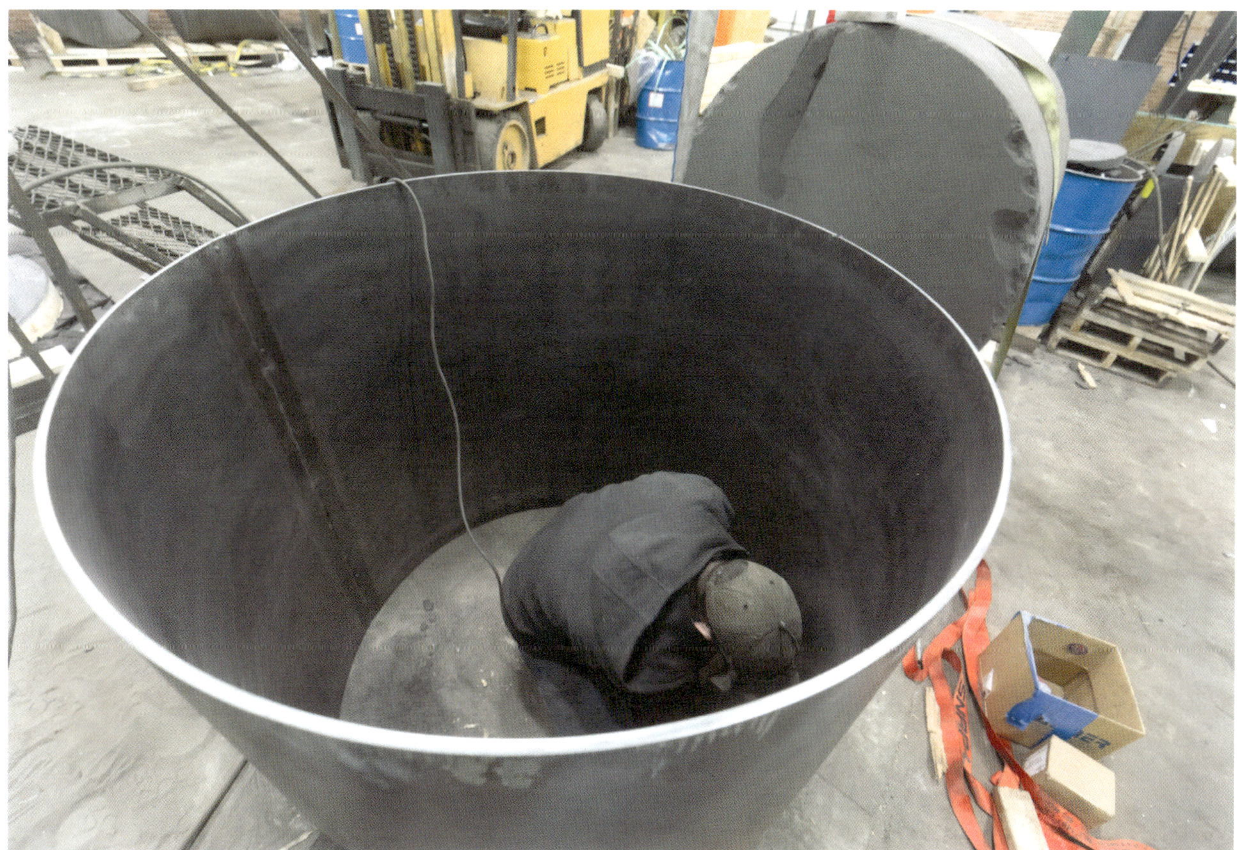

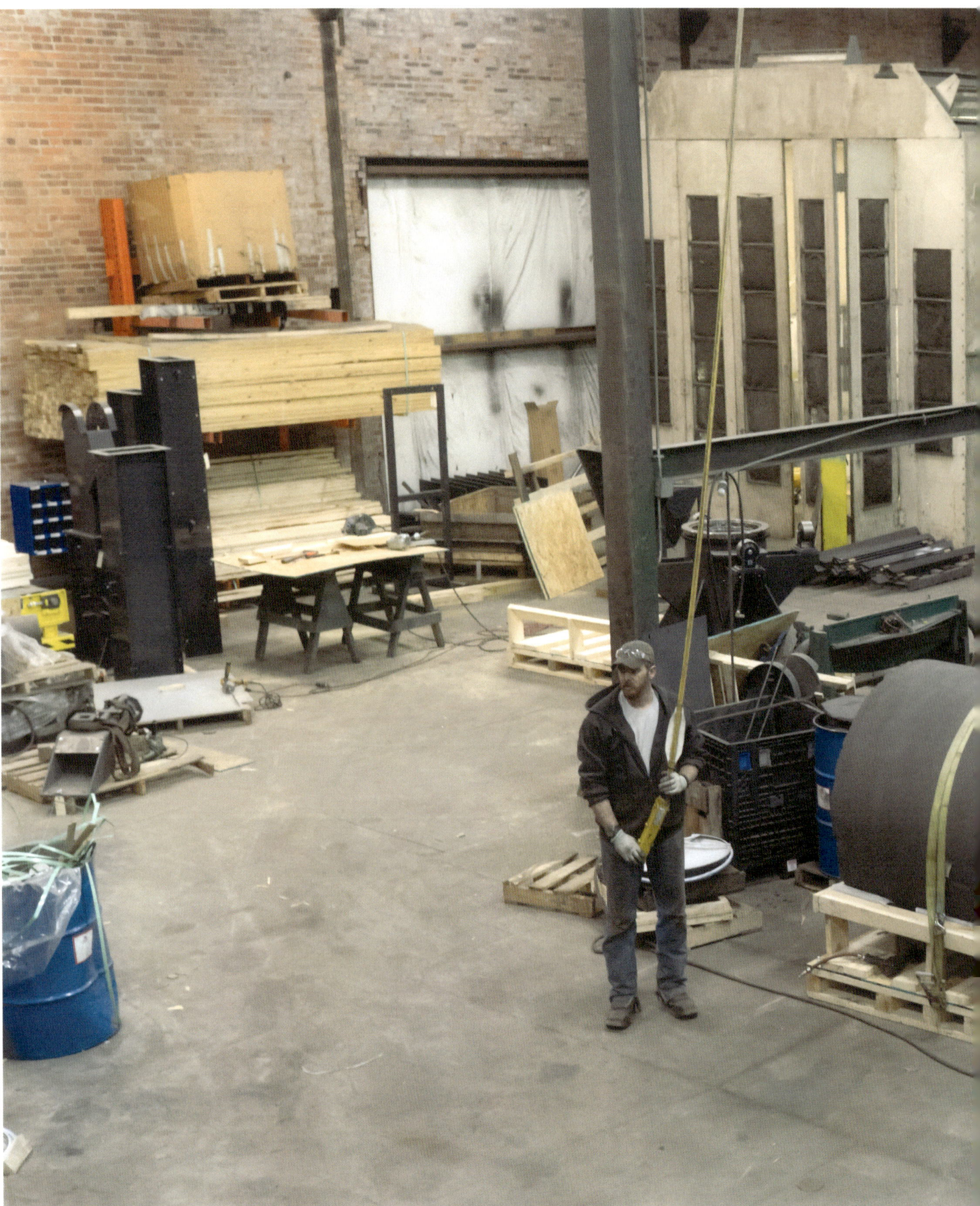

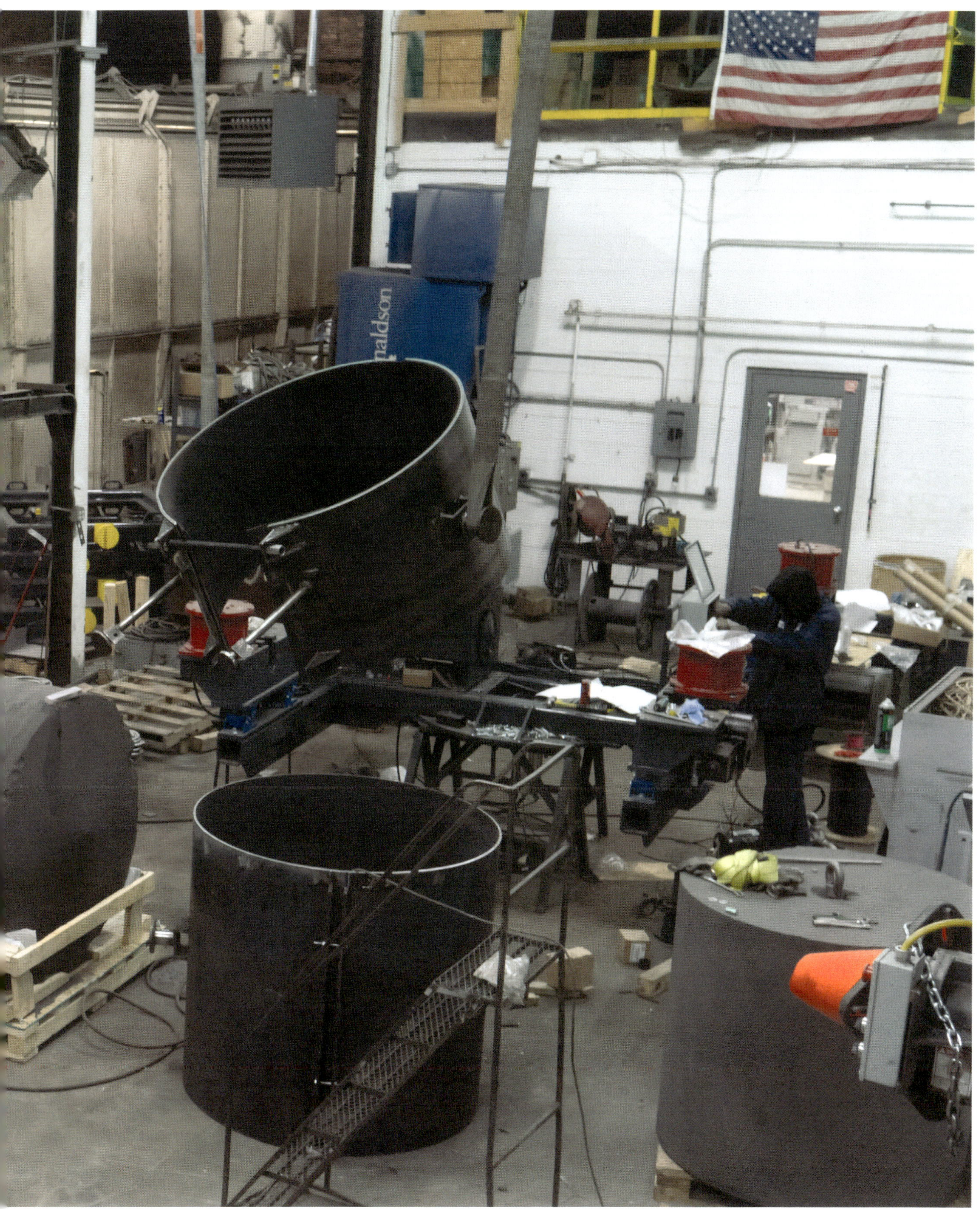

# RELATIVE POINTS

## Installation

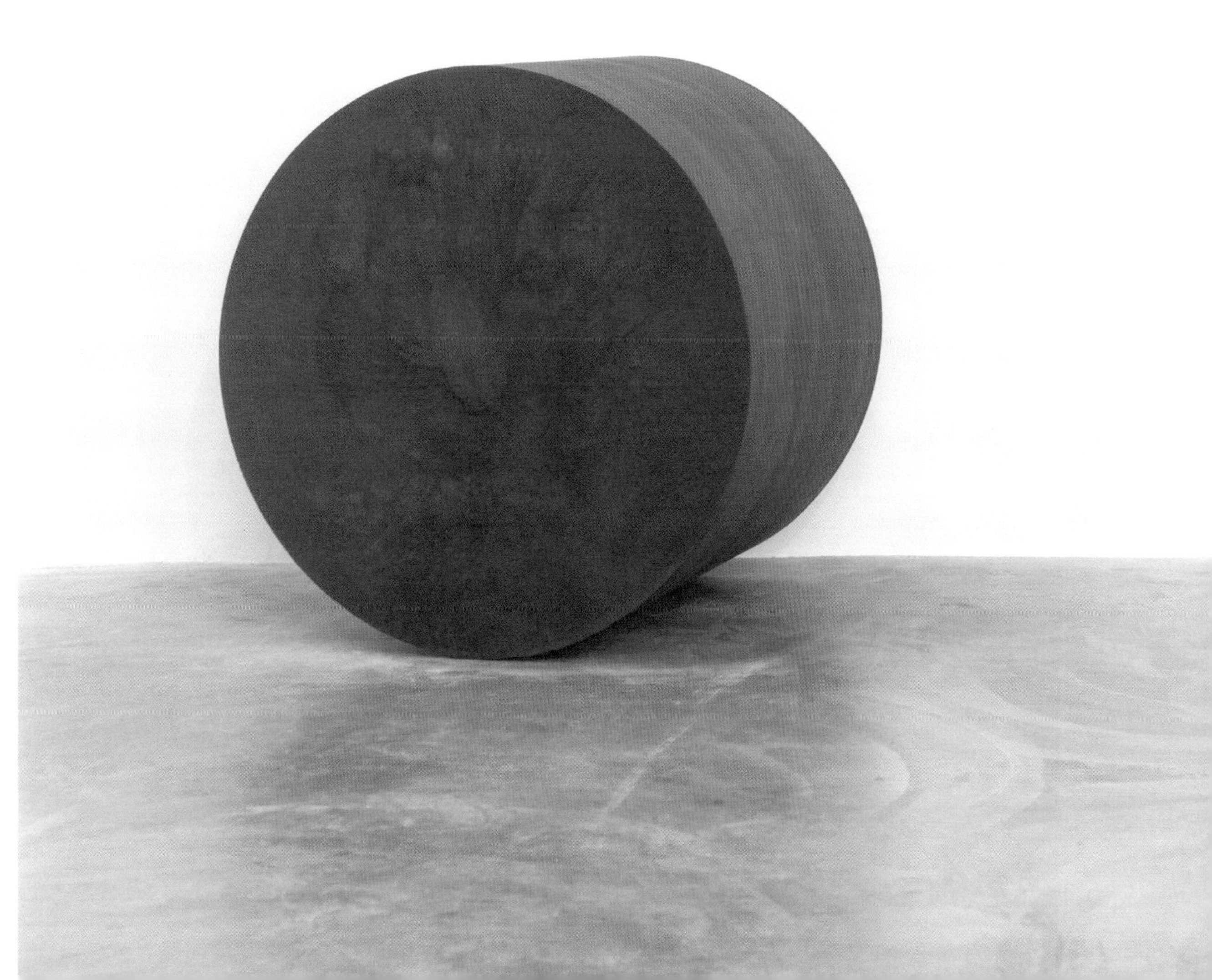

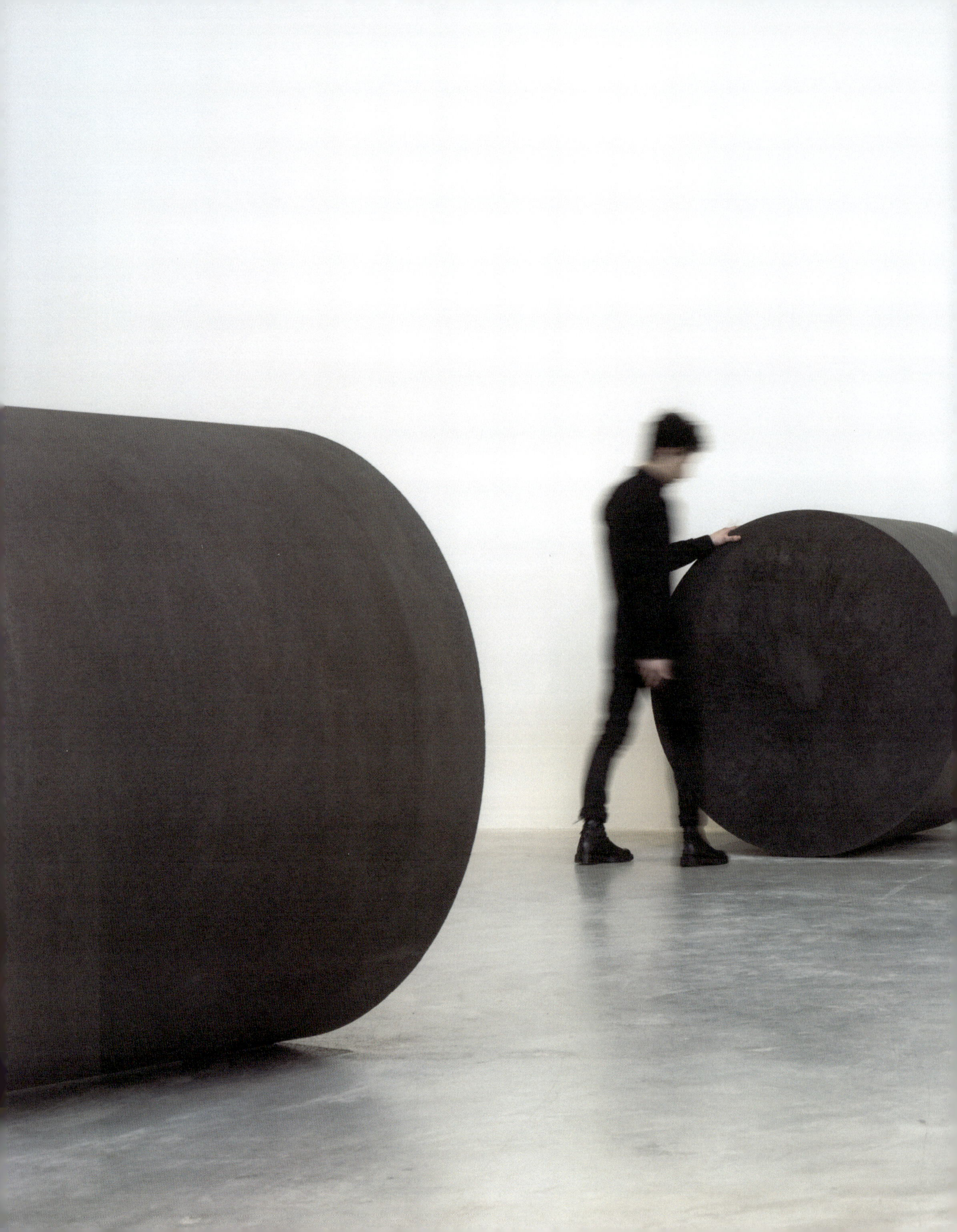

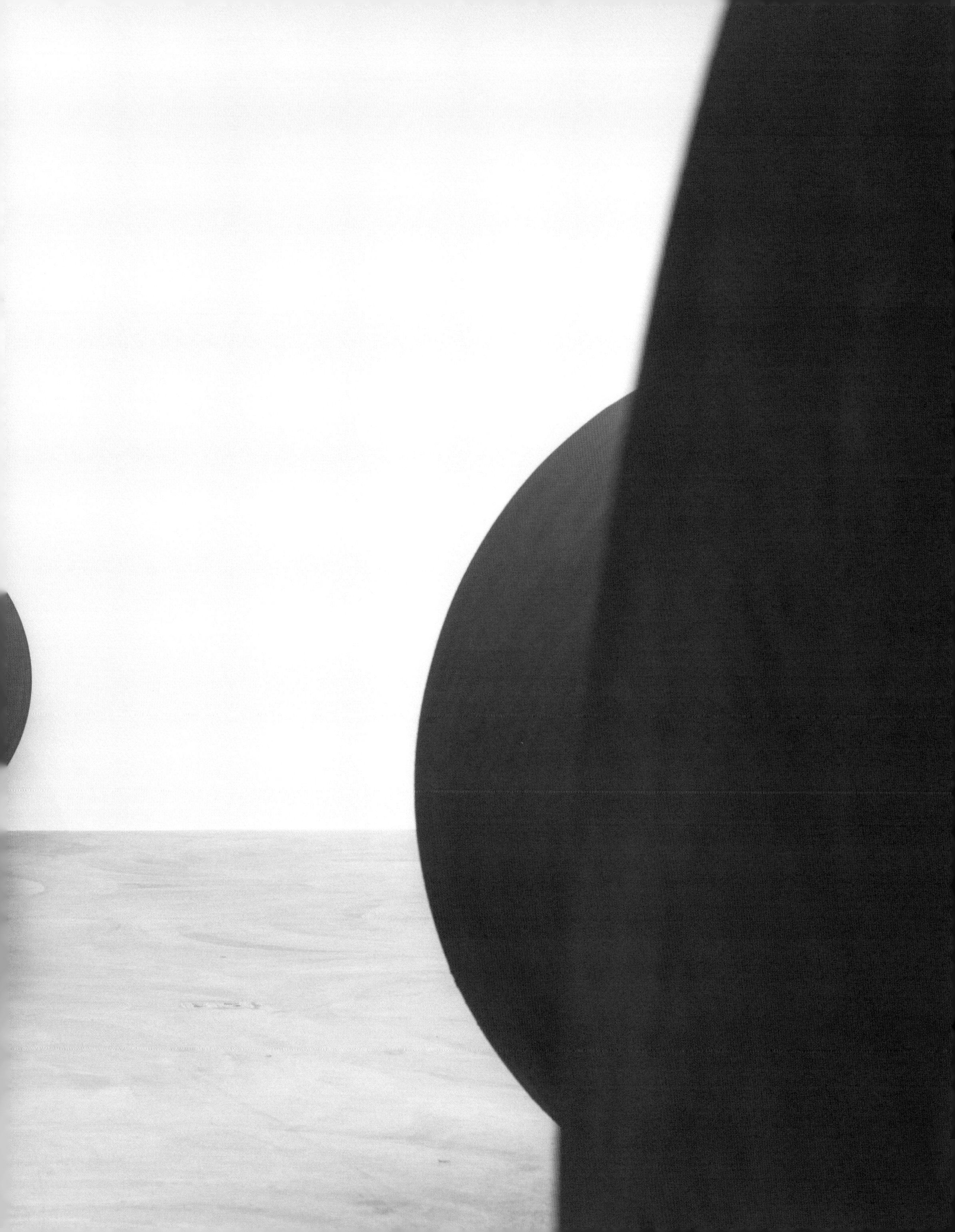

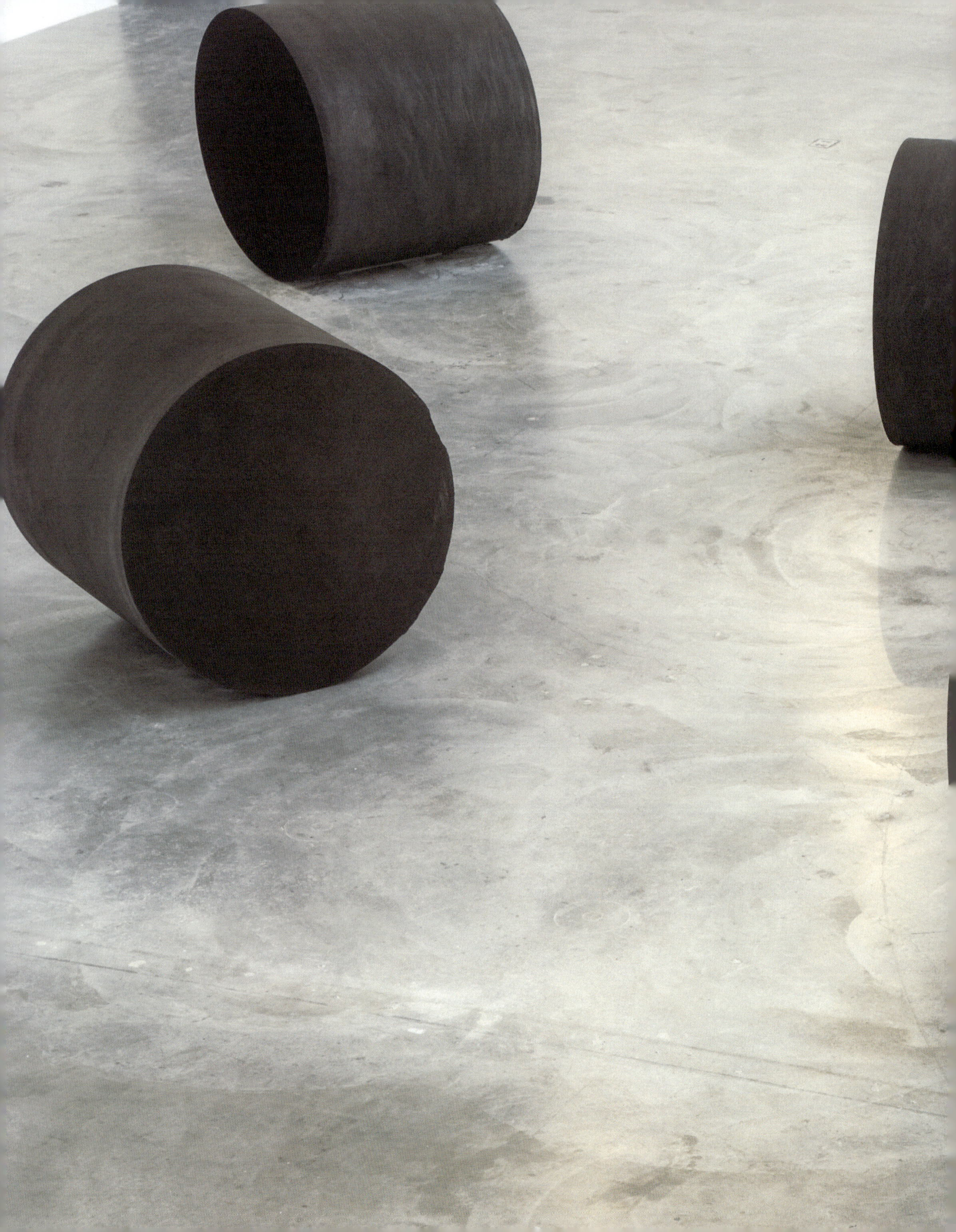

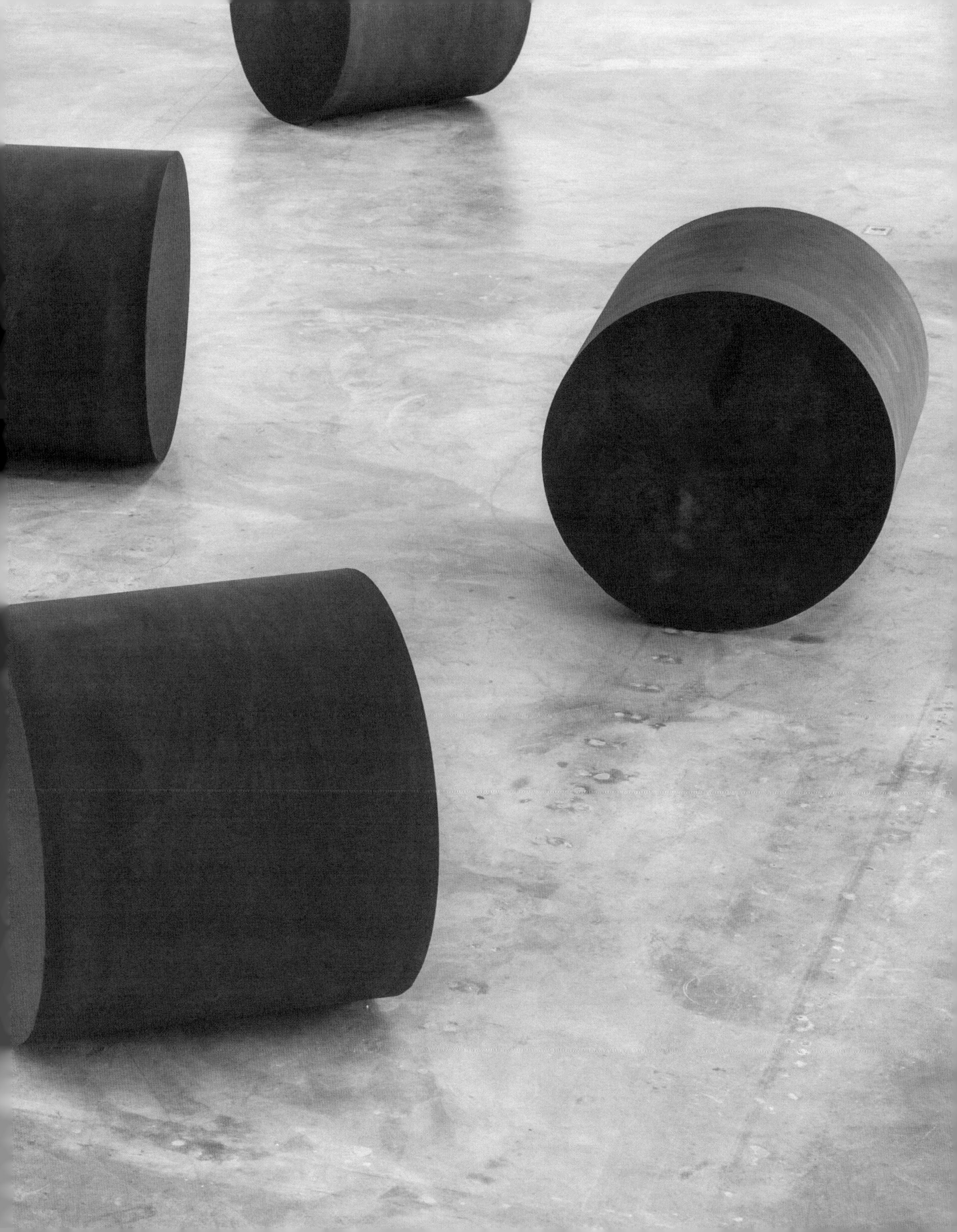

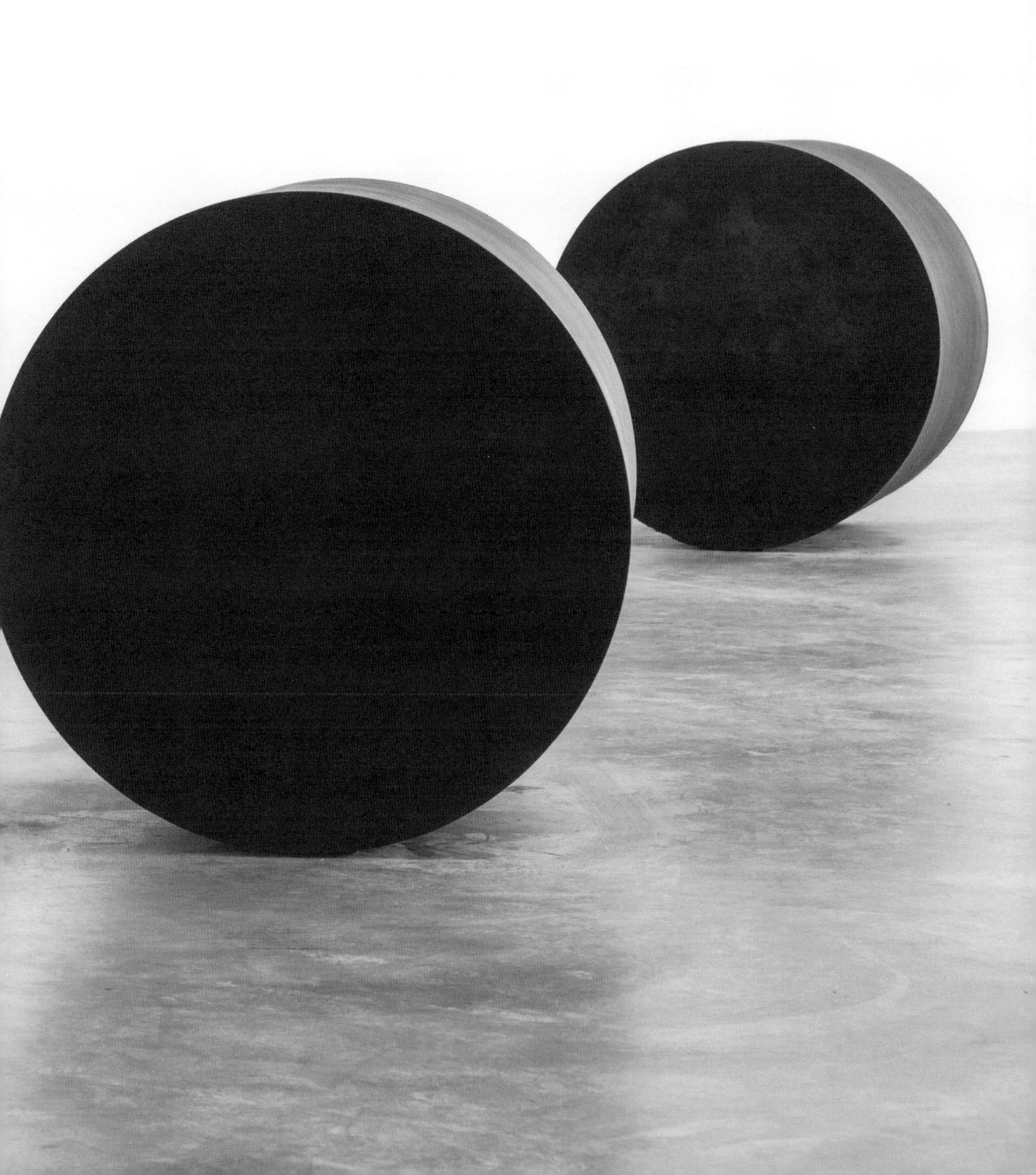

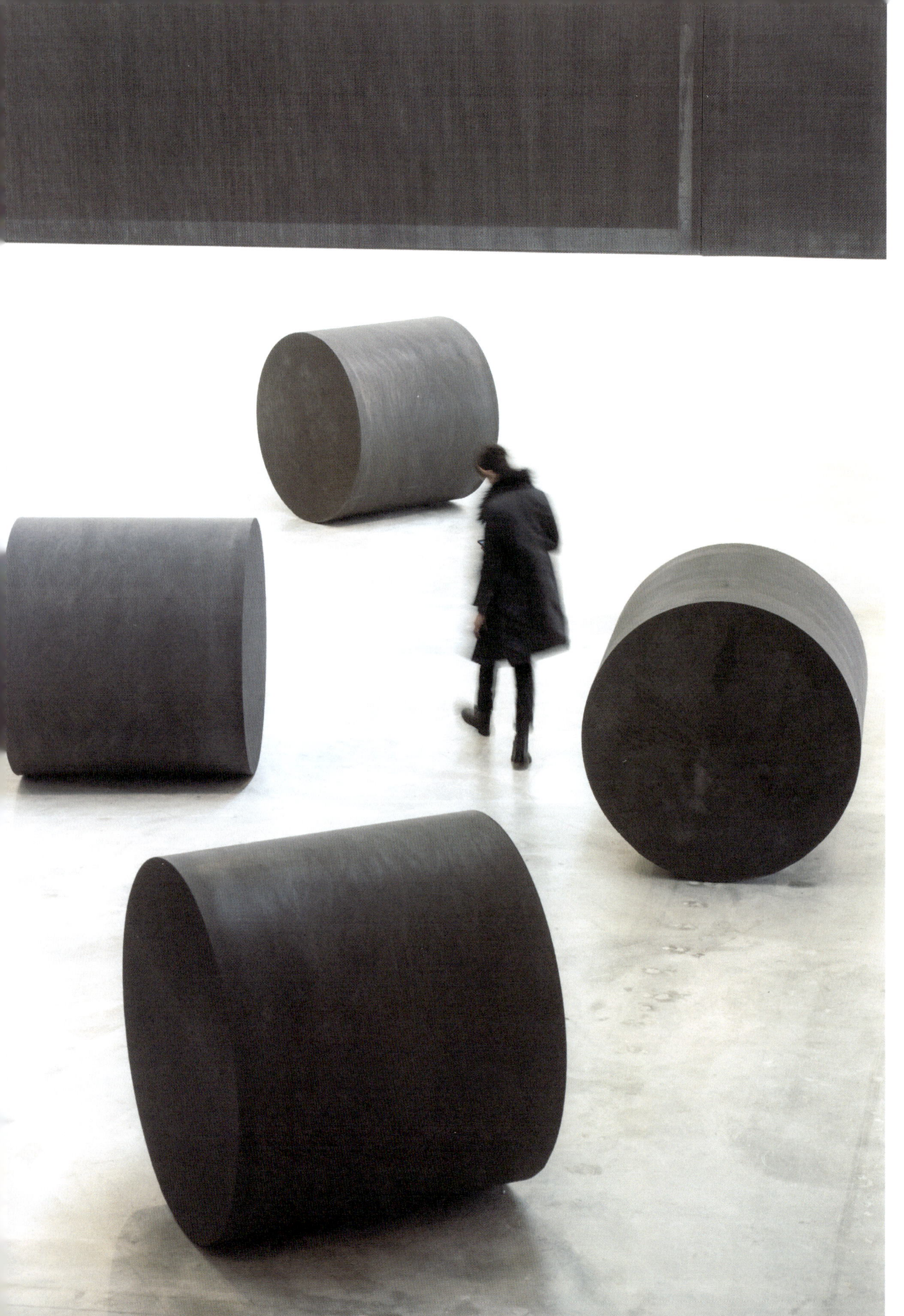

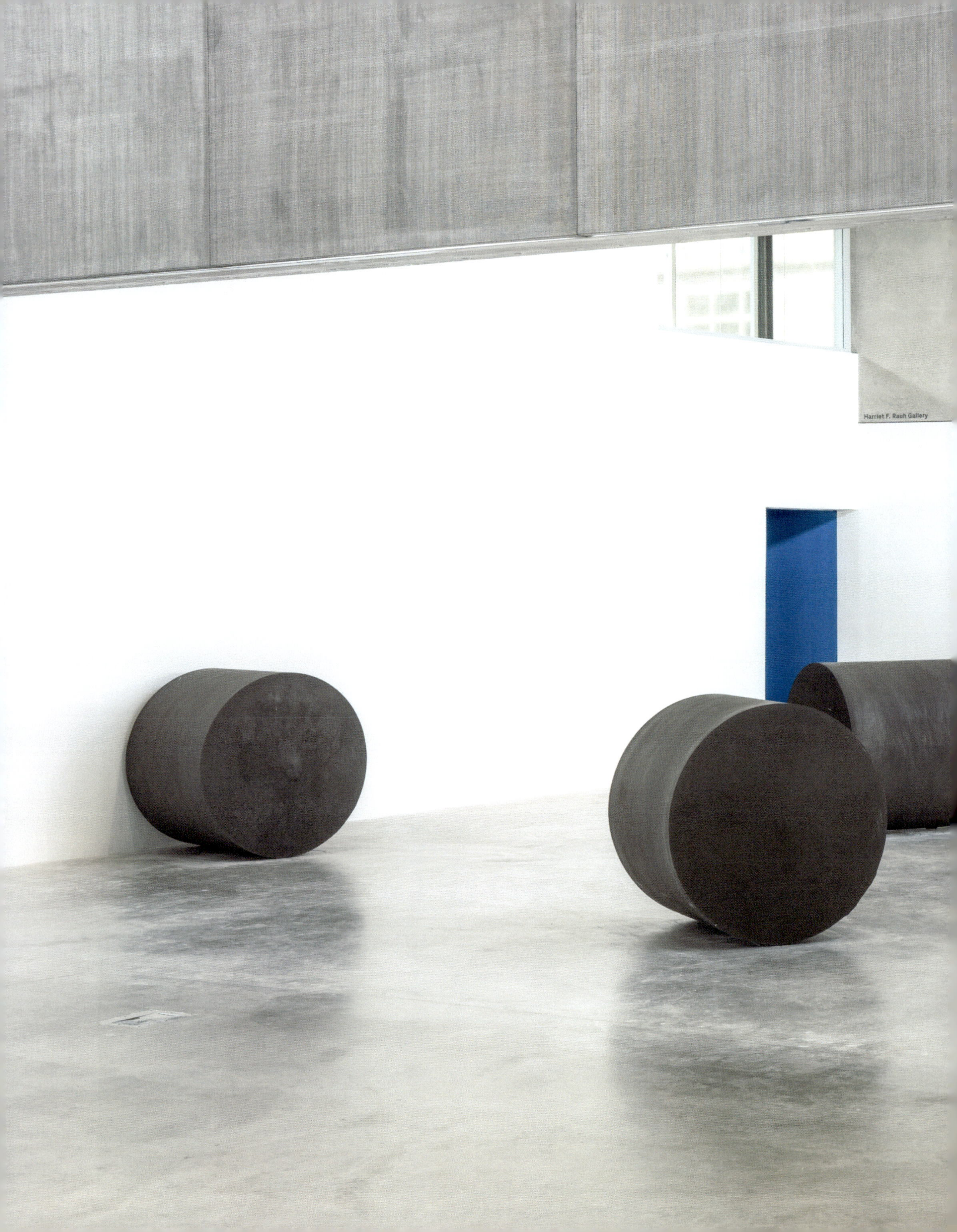
Harriet F. Rauh Gallery

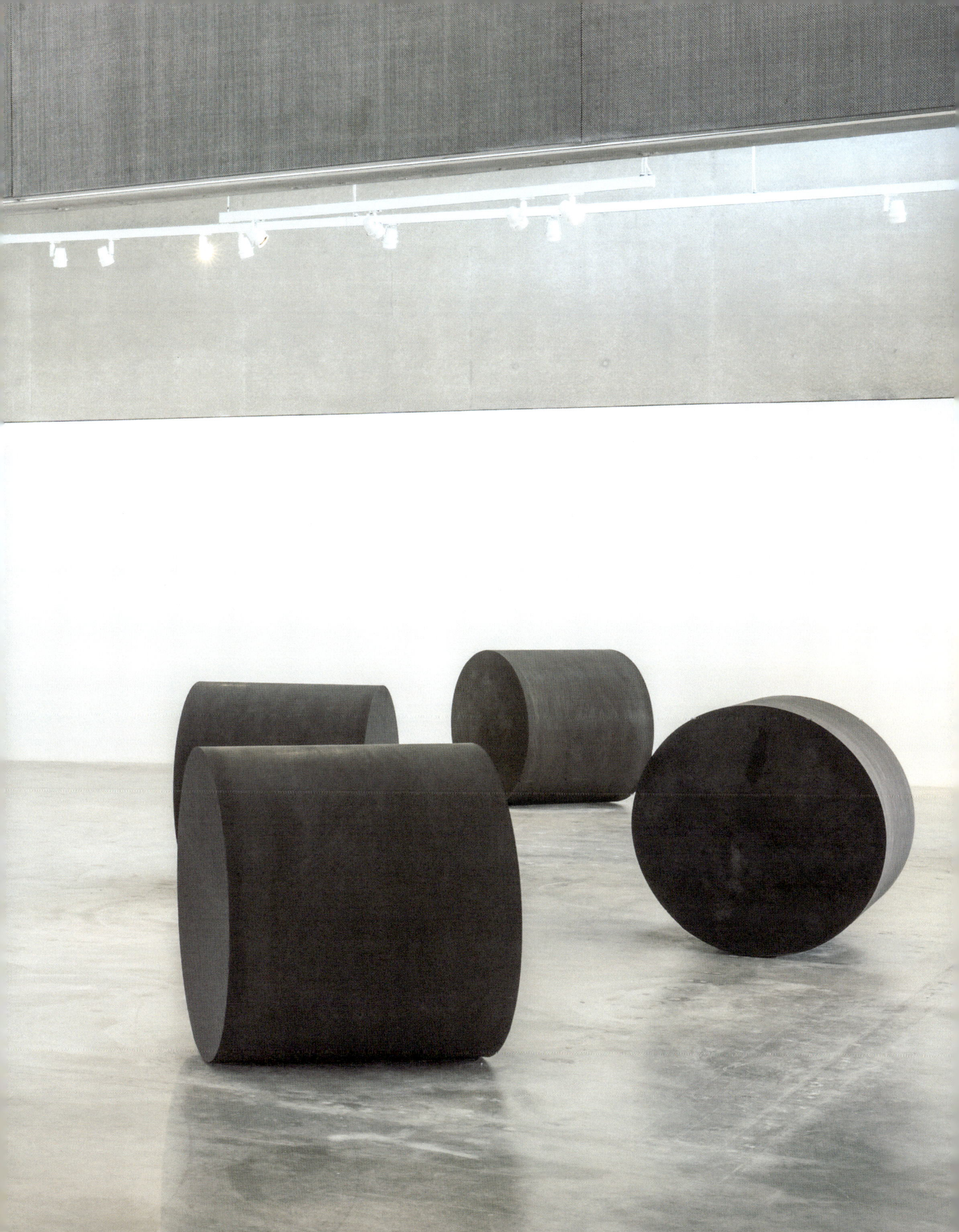

Christine Corday
*Primer Grey, Centers for Gravity 5-4*
2018
Primer paint on aluminum
10 × 8 in.
Photo: Dusty Kessler

Christine Corday
*Primer Grey, Centers for Gravity 5-3*
2018
Primer paint on aluminum
10 × 8 in.
Photo: Dusty Kessler

Christine Corday
*Primer Grey, Centers for Gravity 4-7*
2017
Primer paint on iron
10 × 8 in.
Photo: Dusty Kessler

Christine Corday
*Primer Grey, Centers for Gravity 3-1*
2016
Primer paint on aluminum
10 × 8 in.
Photo: Dusty Kessler

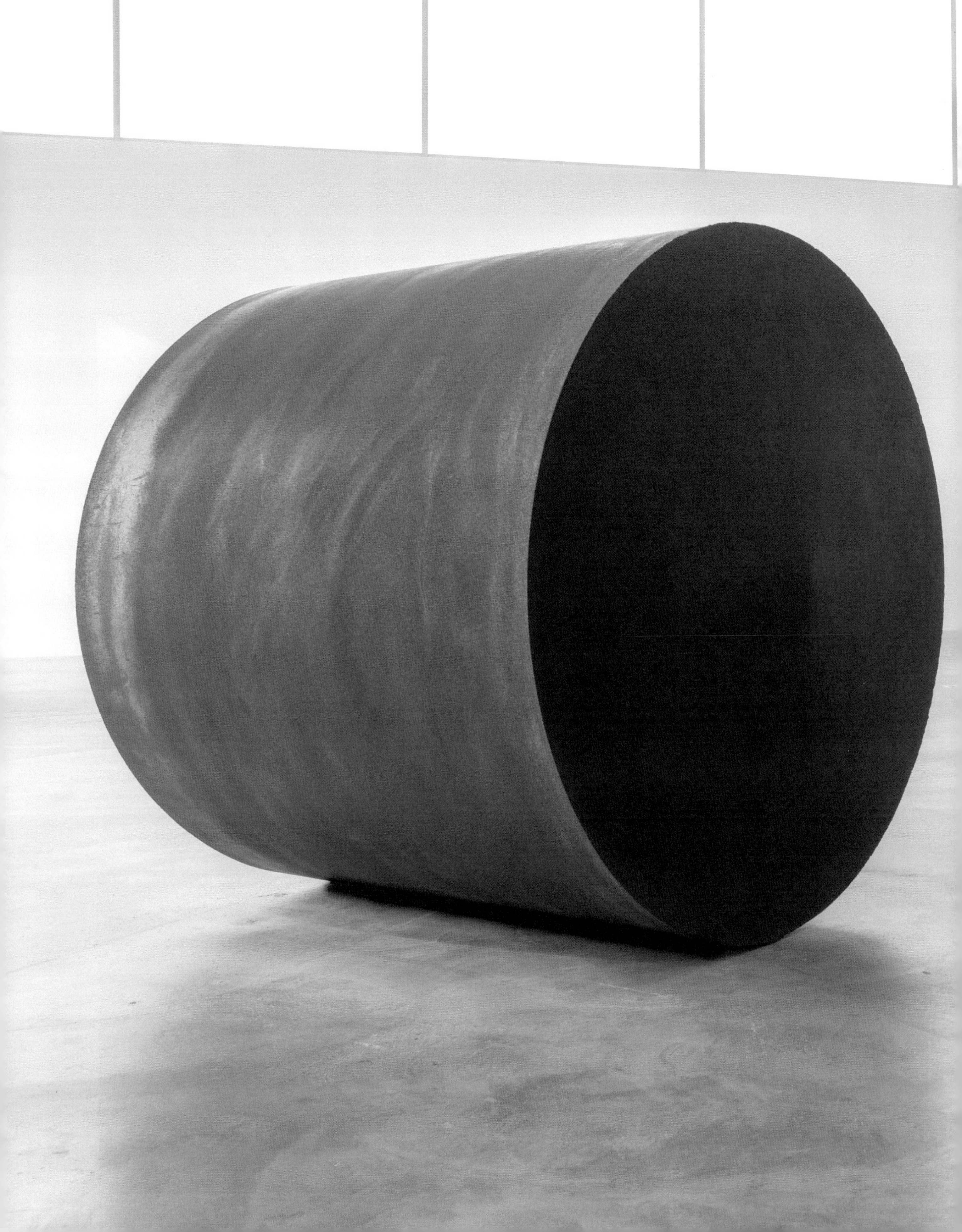

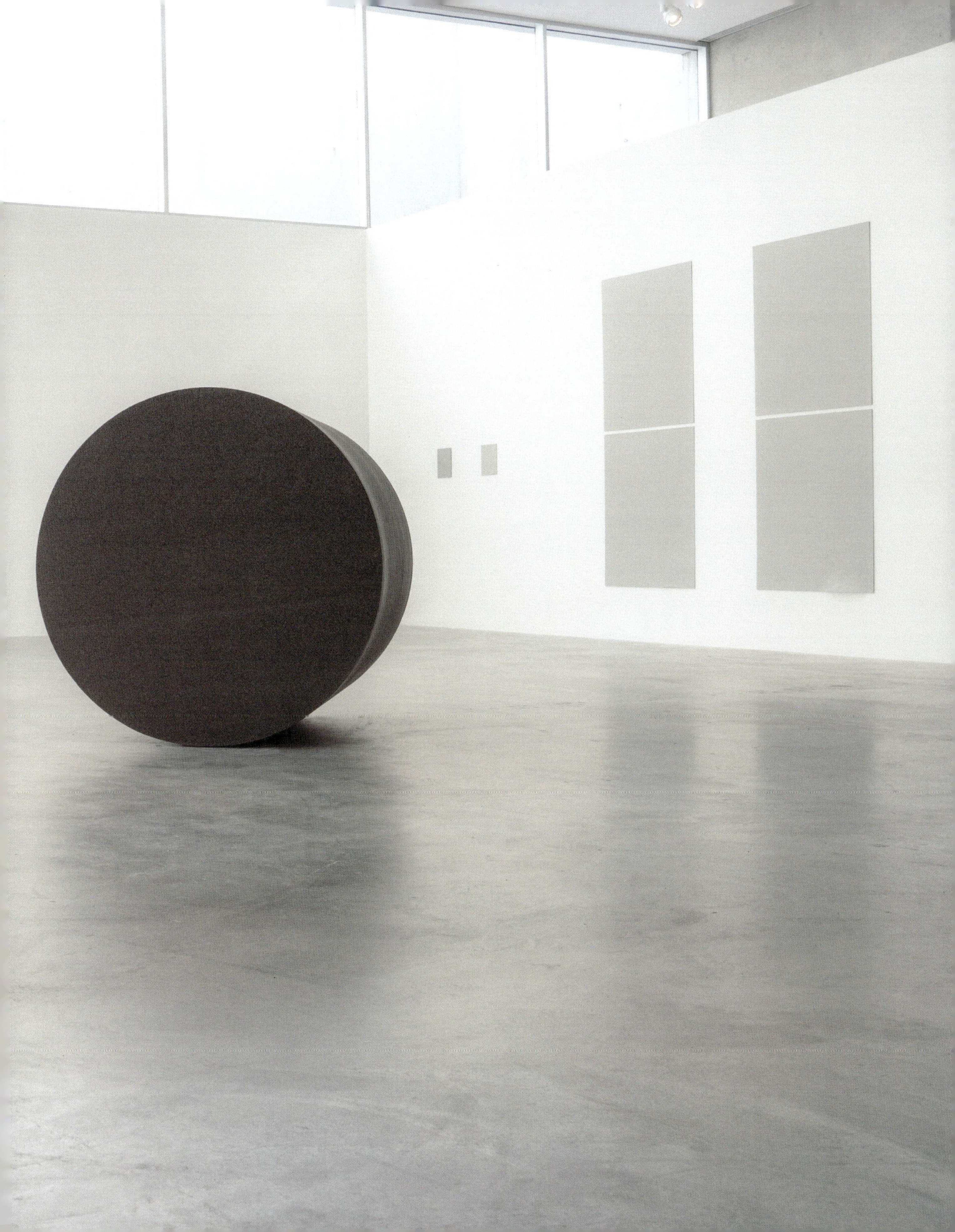

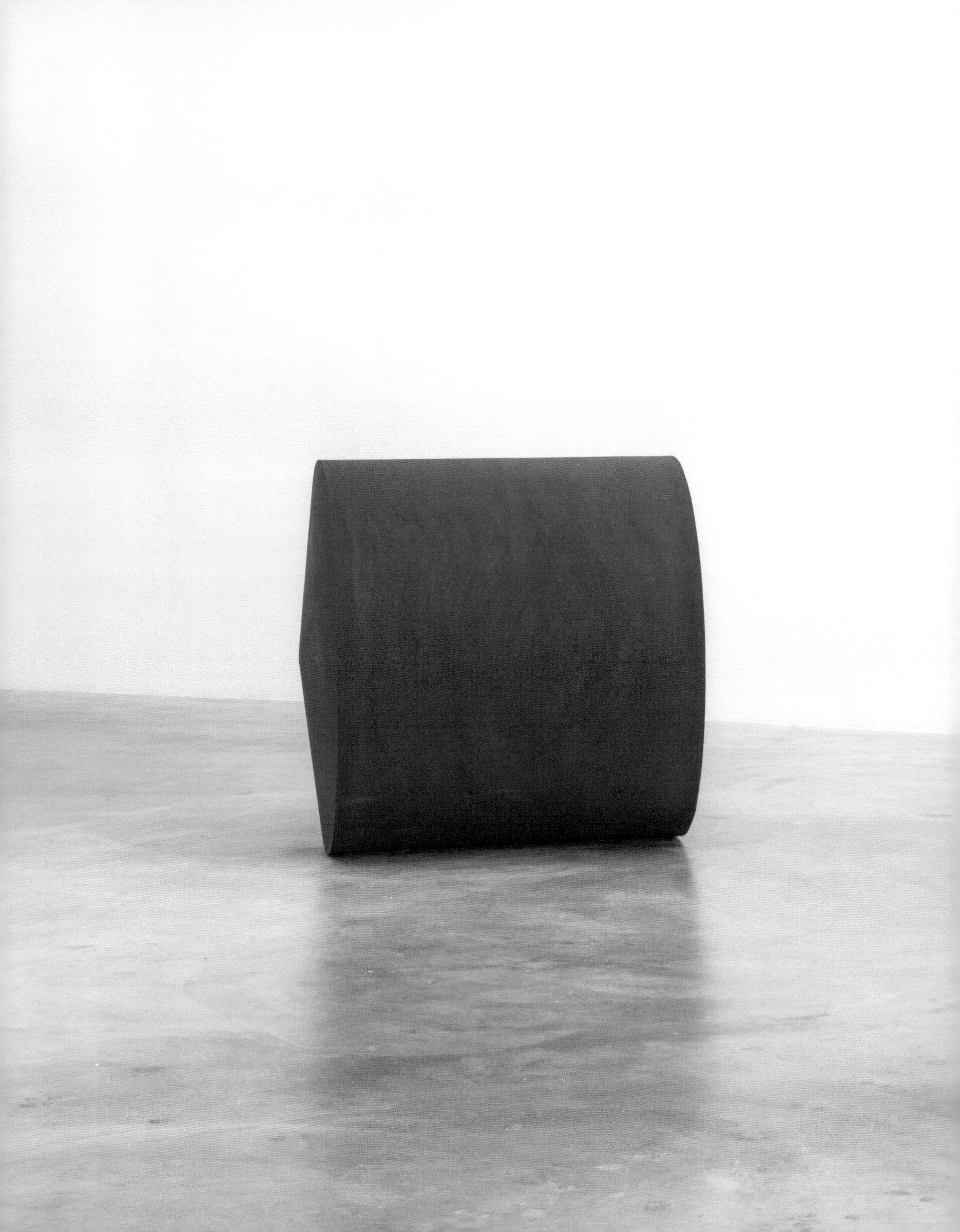

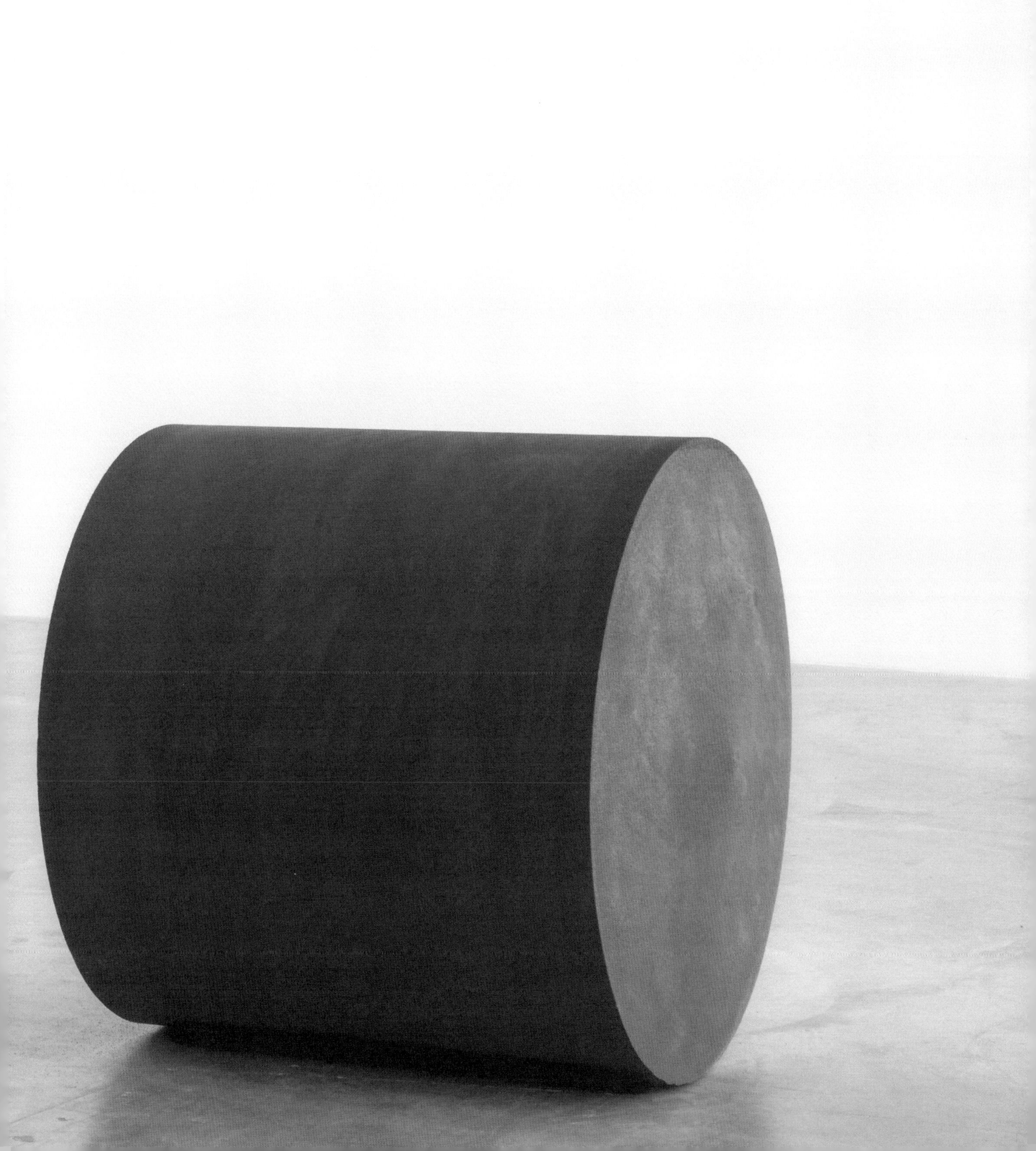

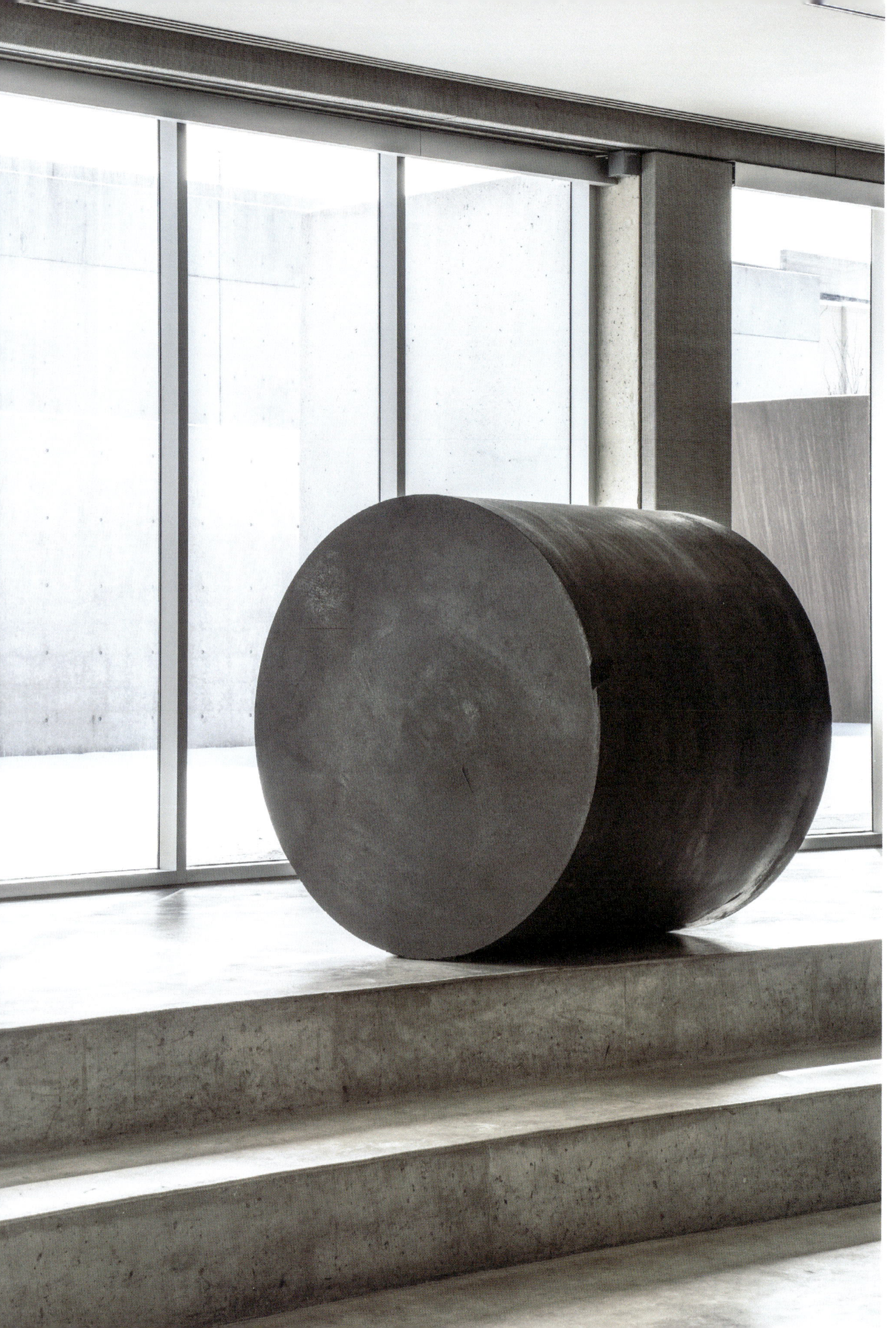

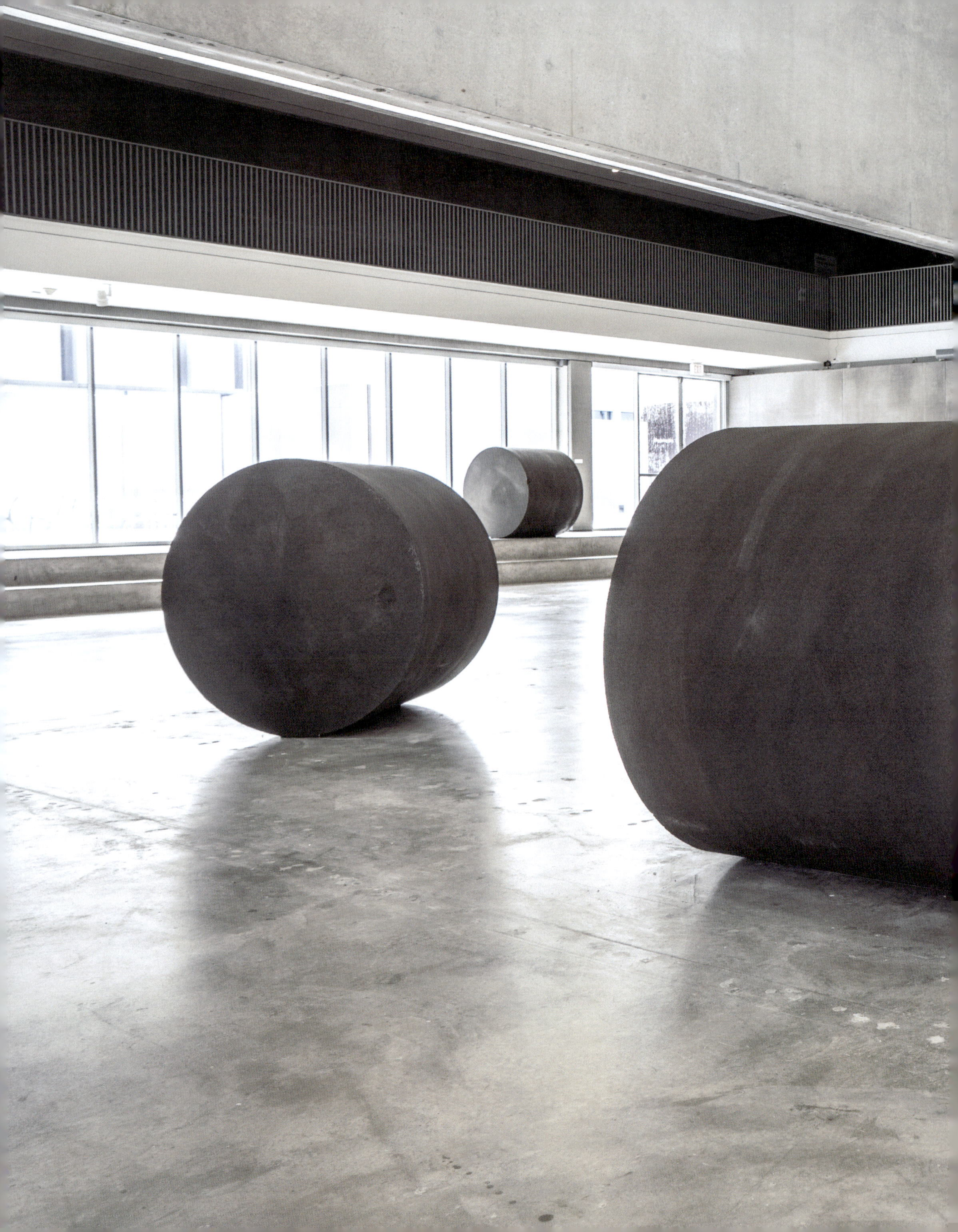

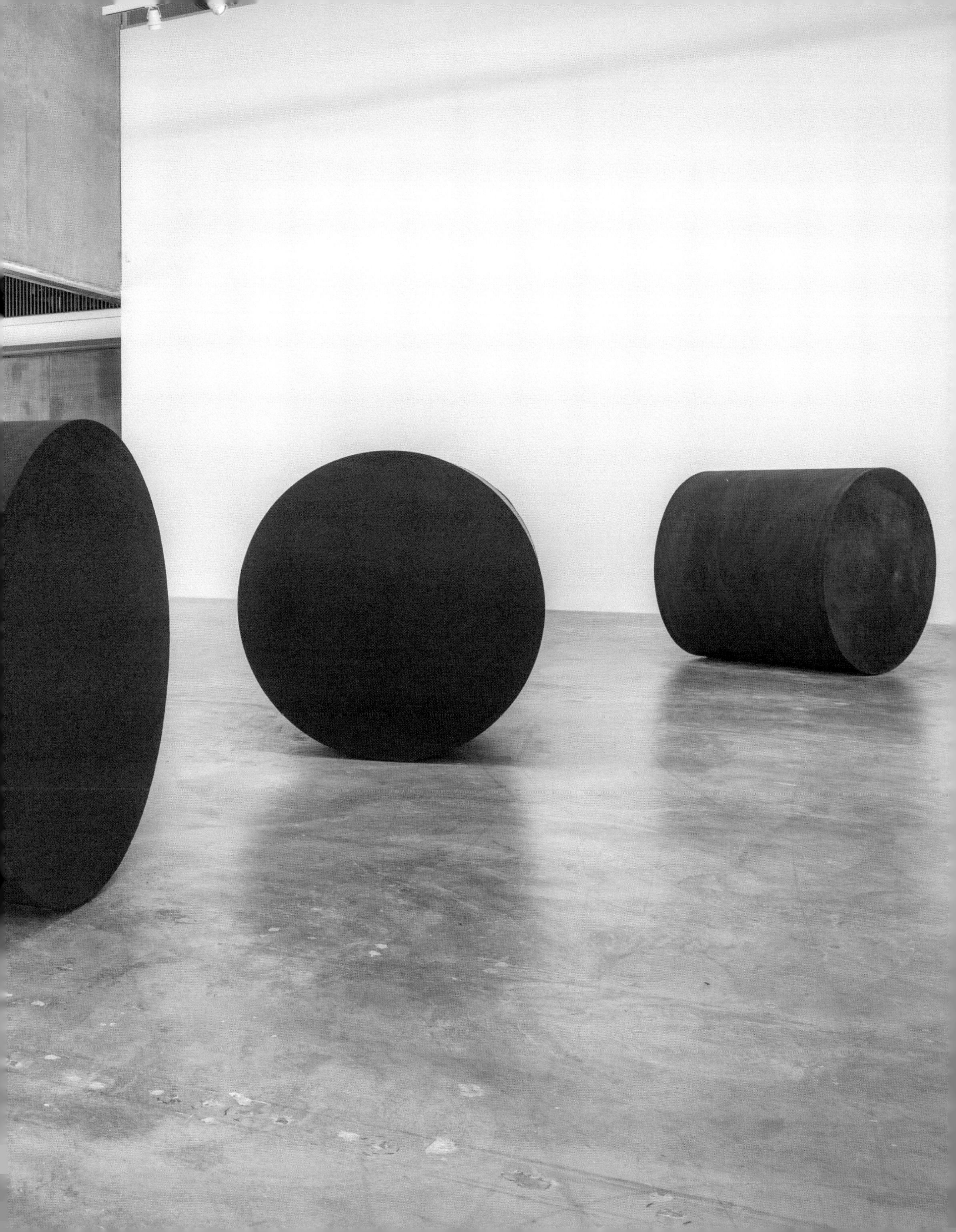

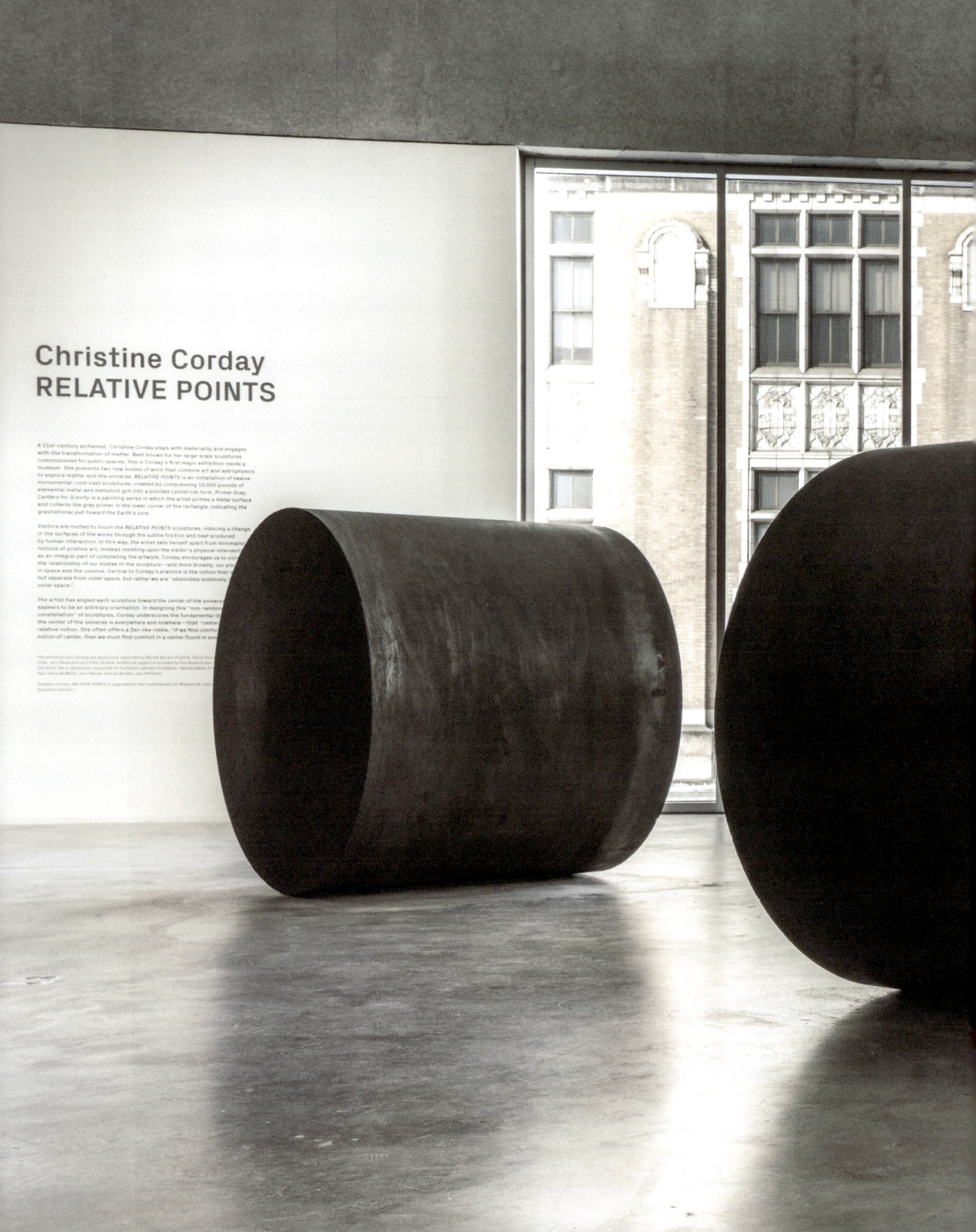
Christine Corday
RELATIVE POINTS
A 21st-century alchemist, Christine Corday plays with materiality and engages with the transformation of matter. Best known for her large-scale sculptures commissioned for public spaces, this is Corday's first major exhibition inside a museum. She presents two new bodies of work that combine art and astrophysics to explore matter and the universe. RELATIVE POINTS is an installation of twelve monumental, cold-cast sculptures, created by compressing 10,000 pounds of elemental metal and metalloid grit into a pointed cylindrical form. Primer Grey, Centers for Gravity is a painting series in which the artist primes a metal surface and collects the grey primer in the lower corner of the rectangle, indicating the gravitational pull toward the Earth's core.

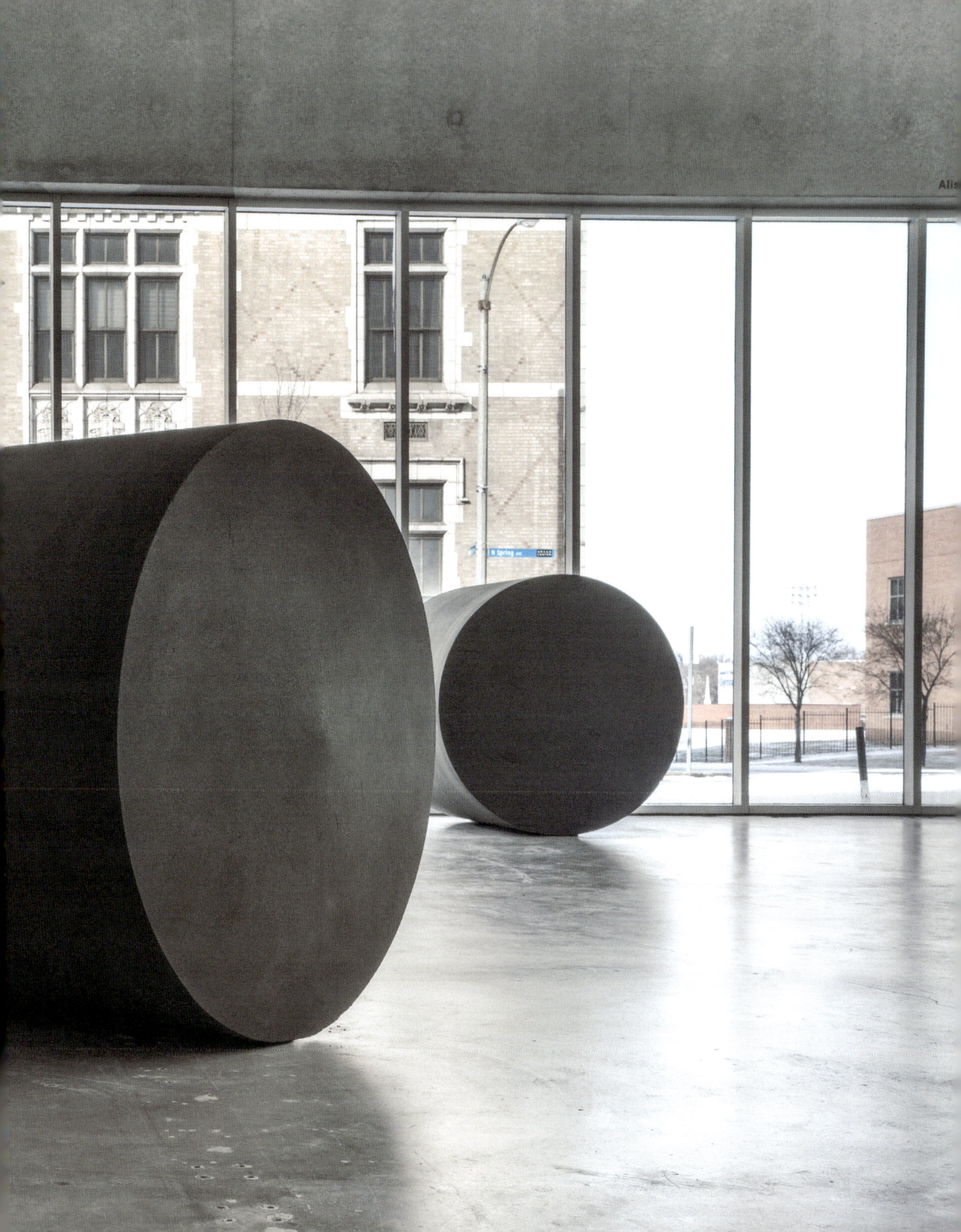
N Spring

# Checklist

*RELATIVE POINTS*, 2018
Iron, metals, metalloids, sodium silicate
53 × 53 × 49 inches each, of 12
Courtesy the artist

*Primer Grey, Centers for Gravity 3-1*, 2016
Primer paint on aluminum
10 × 8 inches
Courtesy the artist

*Primer Grey, Centers for Gravity 4-7*, 2017
Primer paint on iron
10 × 8 inches
Courtesy the artist

*Primer Grey, Centers for Gravity 5-1*, 2018
Primer paint on aluminum
10 × 8 inches
Courtesy the artist

*Primer Grey, Centers for Gravity 5-2*, 2018
Primer paint on aluminum
10 × 8 inches
Courtesy the artist

*Primer Grey, Centers for Gravity 5-3*, 2018
Primer paint on aluminum
10 × 8 inches
Courtesy the artist

*Primer Grey, Centers for Gravity 5-4*, 2018
Primer paint on aluminum
10 × 8 inches
Courtesy the artist

*Primer Grey, Centers for Gravity 6-2*, 2018
Primer paint on aluminum
90 × 36 inches, overall
Courtesy the artist

*Primer Grey, Centers for Gravity 7-1*, 2018
Primer paint on aluminum
90 × 36 inches, overall
Courtesy the artist

# Christine Corday

## b. 1970, Laurel, Maryland

Christine Corday works fluidly between the arts and the sciences. She works with temperature, material states, and elemental metals, often collaborating with international scientists and science organizations. In 1991, before receiving her BA in Communication Arts, she wrote an original research paper that led to an astrophysics internship at NASA Ames Research Center on a SETI extrasolar planetary project. Since then, she has been studying the elements and what makes up our universe: the sun, stars, and elemental particles.

Corday spent part of her childhood in St. Louis and later returned to pursue studies in Cultural Anthropology at Washington University in St. Louis. From 1992–99, she worked as a graphic and structural designer for several international advertising agencies including SKUzzio Design in St. Louis. During this time, she received an Edison Ingenuity Prize in Toronto, as well as international design award for her patented glass bottle for the American tea company The Republic of Tea.

A self-taught artist, Corday devoted herself to painting full-time in 1999 and established her studio abroad in Tokyo, relocating a year later to an attic loft above a flamenco bar in Seville, Spain. There, she created Foundation Civilization for projects exploring the intersections of art and science, such as *Instrument for the Ocean to Play*, which turned tidal energy from the ocean into sound. During her three years in Spain, Corday's palette turned to black, and she began creating works that would come to be seen as blueprints for her future sculptures. The artist started making her own paint by mulling raw pigment and charcoal into a synthetic polymer base to create a tar-like substance, and fabricated tools for its application to raw linen and canvas.

Upon her return to the United States in 2005, she moved to Greenpoint, Brooklyn, and began producing the large metal alloy forms of her *Protoist Series*—massive plasma-cut works focusing on temperature, different material states of elemental metals, and the effect of touch on forms. In 2008, she debuted her first *Protoist* sculpture, a three-ton steel work, *UNE*, under the High Line in New York City. In the following years she continued to place new *Protoist* forms as intimate public encounters in the city.

In 2010, architect Michael Arad and the Memorial Committee selected the black iron oxide color, which Corday formulated in Spain, for the National September 11 Memorial at One World Trade Center in New York City. For nine months, Corday and her assistant applied her blackening color and technique over the 15,000 square feet of the Memorial for its opening on September 11, 2011.

Corday's first solo museum exhibition, *Protoist Series, Selected Forms*, was presented at the Los Angeles County Museum of Art in 2014. Since that time, the artist was nominated for the United States Artist Fellow and received the 2019 Pollock-Krasner Foundation's Brian Wall Foundation Grant for Sculptors. Corday completed two major public art commissions: *FJORWARD* (2016) for Peekskill Landing at the Hudson River, New York, and *GENESES* (2019) for the City of San Francisco at the Moscone Center. Her exhibition at the Contemporary Art Museum St. Louis marked her first solo exhibition inside a museum and was awarded a grant from the National Endowment for the Arts. The exhibition also debuted her first cold-cast iron sculptures, formed through extreme compression rather than heat.

Corday is currently in art and science collaborations with ENBIO in Dublin, Ireland, utilizing its SolarBlack pigment used for the European Space Agency solar orbiter satellite. She is also working with Zybek Advanced Products in Boulder, Colorado, on a new series of works. She will be the first artist to use Zybek's U.S. Geological Survey/NASA plasma tool, which replicates the heat and energy of meteoric impacts. Corday is the sole artist among thousands of scientists from thirty-five nations involved in the ambitious ITER project in Saint-Paul-lez-Durance, France, which seeks to realize a momentary miniature star on Earth. She is also collaborating with UCLA Astrophysics Chair Dr. Andrea Ghez and Keck Observatory on a project casting metal atoms in the upper layer of the Earth's atmosphere.

Corday currently lives and works in Gardiner, New York, with her husband and collaborator, Christopher Powers, and their dog, Rook.

Misa Jeffereis
Assistant Curator

Published on the occasion of the exhibition
*Christine Corday: RELATIVE POINTS*
Contemporary Art Museum St. Louis
January 18–April 21, 2019

Organized by Lisa Melandri, Executive Director, with the assistance of Misa Jeffereis, Assistant Curator

This project is supported in part by an award from the National Endowment for the Arts.

NATIONAL ENDOWMENT for the ARTS
arts.gov

The exhibition and catalog are generously supported by Barrett Barrera Projects, Penny Pennington and Michael Fidler, and Alexandria and Peter Strelow. Additional support is provided by Ann Ruwitch and John Fox Arnold. The Artist Talk is generously supported by the Robert Lehman Foundation. Special thanks to Christopher Powers, Paul Henry McMahill, Jack Palmer, George Murello, and Jeff Hartz.

CONTEMPORARY ART MUSEUM
ST. LOUIS
3750 Washington Boulevard
Saint Louis, Missouri 63108
United States
camstl.org



ISBN-13: 978-0-9977364-1-0
ISBN-10: 0-9977364-1-0

Available through
D.A.P./Distributed Art Publishers
75 Broad Street, Suite 630
New York, NY 10004
212.627.1999
artbook.com

Produced by Lucia | Marquand, Seattle
luciamarquand.com

Editor: Lisa Melandri
Assistant Curator and Catalog Production Manager: Misa Jeffereis
Designer: Meghann Ney
Copy editor: Melissa Duffes
Proofreader: Barbara Bowen
Printer: The Advertisers Printing Company, St. Louis
Installation photographer: Dusty Kessler (pp. cover image, 2–3, 11, 14, 17, 29, 33, 55, 56–57, 58–59, 60–61, 62–63, 64, 66–67, 68–69, 70, 71, 72–73, 74–75, 76, 78–79, 80–81)